Published by Lewarne Publis

PO Box 26946

London SE21 8X(

England

www.lewarnepublishing.co.uk

ISBN 978-0-9513168-6-3

First published 1.9.07

Front/back cover design by Yasha-H, London
Typesetting by MKG, Bridgwater
Printed by Kampress, Bridgwater, Somerset, England

Foreword by Lord Robert Baden-Powell

I am pleased to have been asked to write a foreword to Steven Harris's very original biography of my grandfather and history of the UK Scout Movement.

Baden-Powell was a man of his times and was influenced by his social and physical environment. He was the right person, at the right time with the most benevolent influences to encourage him to work out a method of self-help for what were then known as the working classes. Baden-Powell based his ideas on the natural inclination of young people who were in fear of the adult world and so sought the safety of numbers in their contemporaries - the gang or patrol. Anyone else at any other time in history would not have had the influences or background to have thought out what was, at the time, a revolutionary system for personal social enlightenment.

Baden-Powell was born in the middle of the 19th century into a highly literate family from the professional class (his father being the mathematician who formulated the binary system - the lifeblood of the modern computer), and his life reflects his family's concern for their less privileged compatriots. One of his brothers, concerned at the poor living conditions of people in our great industrial cities put a bill through Parliament whereby £1 procured a Government assisted passage to Canada, Natal, Australia or New Zealand. The consequences of this Act have been profound for those countries and the UK. Another brother worked on first spotting kites and balloons suspended 300 feet above the battleship and then, when motors had become powerful enough for flight, using aircraft catapulted off the ships. He was heavily involved in the development of the aircraft carrier. A further brother, concerned at the logistics of trying to get armies around countries with no railways, invented a folding bicycle to help foot soldiers. Two million of them went to the Front during the Great War - where they proved useless in the mud! His oldest brother, a keen sailor, wished to bring his hobby to ordinary people so developed the sailing canoe (cheap to buy and easy to transport and store).

Baden-Powell was amongst the first intake of professional Officers from his class rather than from the landed gentry. He was an original thinking tactician whose prime concern was winning and, secondarily, the well-being of the men under his command. After many years in the army he was placed on the reserve list and took a substantial cut in his army stipend. To mitigate this it was suggested that he update for general sale a small booklet he had written for army recruits called 'Aids to Scouting'. Little did he know that the book, transformed into 'Scouting for Boys', would have such profound consequences for millions of boys of all classes, for generations to come.

It is lucky for many millions of people around the world that Baden-Powell was born when he was and came from such an enlightened family background. His ideas are now entrenched in educational thinking and will survive and help young people to become well adjusted for many years into the future.

Lord Baden-Powell, August 2007

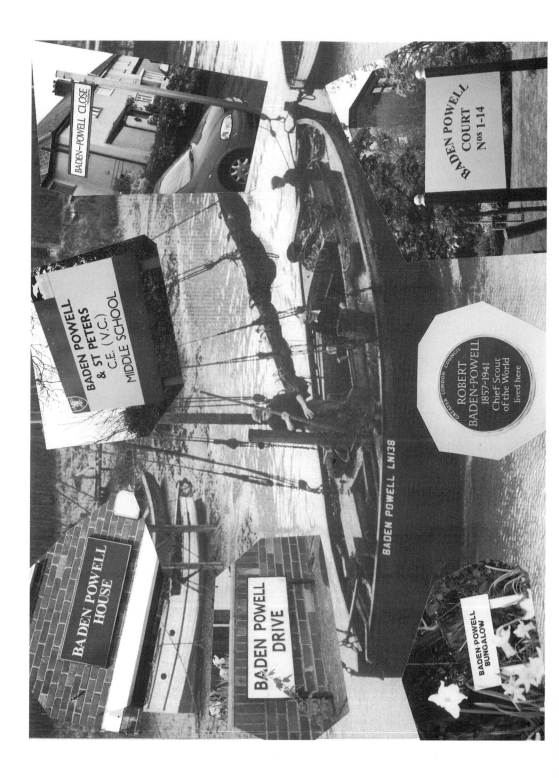

CONTENTS

CONTENTS SECTION TWO

~~~~ REFERENCE SECTION ~~~~

INTRODUCTION

Historians have called him the 'boy-man'. He was certainly a one-off, an original and someone who championed the boy, especially those from a less privileged background. Scouting's founder, Lord Baden-Powell, was no bright scholar from a rich family, he became a hands-on idol with unique ideas that are still copied to this day. Indeed, he became something of a charismatic figure even before he found fame under Lord Roberts during the South African War (notably for his part in the siege of Mafeking). Promoted the youngest Major-General in the army, he would land up spending 34 years as a soldier and 34 years as the leader of the Boy Scout movement. His Boy Scout idea, started as an experimental camp on Brownsea Island, was originally offered as something to spice up existing boys' organisations' programmes. His scheme grew to millions of boys making it their own: turning it into an amazing youth phenomenon of the twentieth century.

It is a world-wide youth movement today with over 28 million Scouts. Aspects of the movement have been woven into the very canvas of our society with well-worn images and vocabulary. Shorts, often called knickers in 1907, became normal wear for all boys after they were worn by Boy Scouts. Such terms as 'Posse', 'Scout's honour', 'Bob-a-job' and 'dyb dyb dyb', although not used in the Scouts for decades, are still a fondly stored part of our language that are brought out for an occasional airing. The likes of Russ Abbott, Ronnie Barker and Ronnie Corbett, along with countless other comedians, couldn't resist the lure of the woggle (not toggle!) and big hat, incorporating them in their sketches.

By the 1970s one in every four British males had been in the Scouts at one time in their lives, and whilst it is not as big as it once was in the UK, the movement world-wide continues to grow. Household names such as Sir John Major, Sir Richard Branson and Michael Owen were all in the Scouts (and royalty: Lord Snowdon and Prince Andrew) - it had enormous appeal to a wide cross-section of male youth. So along with the likes of former Scouts Val Doonican, Sir Cliff Richard (okay for one day only!) and Sir Trevor Brooking, the Scouts opened its doors and held appeal for rock-band Slade drummer Don Powell, Boy George, Jeffrey Archer and Jim Davidson. Alas Scouting was unable to help keep all boys on the straight and narrow: murderer John Christie - of 10 Rillington Place fame - had been one of the country's first Boy Scouts and rose to become an Assistant Scoutmaster.

Former Scoutmasters/leaders in the movement include B.-P.'s wife, Olave, B.-P.'s grandson (who started as a humble Group Scoutmaster in Putney), Lord Soper, Richard Baker and former Prime Minister Harold Macmillan. Further afield, the first man to set foot on the Moon, Neil Armstrong, was an Eagle Scout and Scout leader. Long before equality laws, the Scouts ran Troops for disabled children (later integrated with able-bodied Scouts), allowed female Scoutmasters, and during the 1930s the movement gained its first blind Scoutmaster (others followed).

Not that it could always capture the minds or wishes of all boys. A well known Mayor once 'confessed' on a BBC radio programme to getting no nearer to joining the Scouts than smashing a scout hut window in his native Tulse Hill. Hugh Dennis, one half of the comedy duo Punt and Dennis, although being the son of a vicar, was drummed out of the Wolf Cubs despite it being attached to his father's church. He was also bitterly disappointed to find that his collection of recorded number plates did not qualify him for the Collector badge! Playwright Alan Bennett was relatively successful in the Wolf Cubs but never made the transition to the school Scout Troop. In correspondence with the author he explained why:

It's true I never graduated to the Scouts because you had to be able to skip backwards 30 times, a skill I never mastered. I'm sure the skipping, though, was just the tip of the ice-berg and many other incapacities would soon have been revealed.

Of course, there have been numerous histories of the Scout movement and biographies on Baden-Powell before, some approaching eulogies, others overly critical (and invariably inaccurate). A comprehensive one and the most reliable to date is that by Tim Jeal. In the book you are reading, therefore, I have not attempted to reinvent the wheel. 'A Quirky Biography' is intended to be a lighter, briefer read that tells the story of B.-P.'s life and his movement (not to the present day) - aiming to keep in the quirky and more interesting bits. (Since his soldiering days Baden-Powell has always been known as B.-P.)

For numerologists and believers (or disbelievers) of fate or coincidences, watch out! Without much digging there are many quirks of fact, date and number, along with coincidences and near coincidences (these have been presented in bold type throughout the main text). The prime number seven, for example (what some mathematicians refer to, appropriately enough for B.-P., as the 'survivor number'), seems to crop up a lot concerning B.-P., as do his initials and date of birth: 22nd February 1857. Now, as B.-P would say, no more loafing, so get reading!

RSS   8th January

217   17

St. George   July

BP   Robert

22nd February 1857

S. A.   7   seventh

Charterhouse   Wimbledon

Peter   30th October

B.S.A.   1907   17th May

From Boy to Soldier....

It was in the year 1857 when Baden-Powell (B.-P.) was born. Some thirty years before, the composer Beethoven (1770 - 1827) had died. He was born in Bonn, some 170 miles from B.-P.'s namesake Baden in Germany. He wrote nine symphonies, 32 sonatas and much more. For his **Scout M**ovement B.-P. wrote nine Scout laws, published 32 books, and much more. In almost the same year (1858), Emmeline Pankhurst was born. Through the **Suffragette M**ovement she would achieve much for women. Perhaps feminists should look a little harder at what B.-P., with his sister and wife, did for girls and women. Women were accepted into the Scouts - a movement for boys and men; girls as Guides were given licence to leave their sewing and do what the boys were doing: getting their hands dirty through winning badges, rambling, first-aid and camping.

On the 22nd February **1857** Scouting's founder, Robert Stephenson Smyth Powell, was born on the **seventh** day of the week at 6, Stanhope Street, a stone's throw from the northern boundary of Hyde Park, London SW7. As a boy in his first year of life he would have been totally unaware of the Indian mutiny taking place. Queen Victoria had come on to the thrown in 1837 and would be declared Empress of India in **1876**. Little could he or Victoria have guessed that one day they would become well acquainted with each other. Lucknow was under siege in **1857**, and it would be Lucknow that was B.-P.'s first military posting in **1876**. Sieges and soldiering would make him famous before he became a hero again as the founder of the Boy Scout movement.

Back to **1857**, one tends to forget that B.-P. lived for more than half his life in the Victorian period - not all his ideas and influences were Edwardian. His mother, Henrietta, and father, the Reverend Powell, had moved into their Stanhope Street home on the **17th May**, a few years before B.-P.'s birth. Perhaps it was a prophetic day, as the famous siege of Mafeking (where B.-P. first found acclaim) lasted **217** days, and ended on the **17th May** 1900. *The Times* led the way with idolatry accounts of the **B**ritish **P**luck of **B**.-**P**. and his men.

B.-P.'s father, also born on the 22nd (August not February), in **1797**, became Savilian Professor of Geometry at Oxford in 1827. Sadly, he would die when B.-P. was only three. A friend of Darwin, he had become a controversial figure, claiming, for example, that all miracles would be proved by lay means. But on the day of B.-P.'s birth *The Times* had far less to report, though one of its overseas correspondents did write a piece under the name of Brussel Sprouts (page **7**). Soon after the Boy Scout movement's inception in 1907, its young members would occasionally come under siege from young ruffs throwing old potatoes and shouting "Oy, brussel sprouts, yer bleeding, blinking louts!". The **b**russel sprouts - **b**oy **s**couts - were rather conspicuous in their shorts and big hats, so to join them often demanded steely nerves.

In B.-P.'s youth there was little for boys to do. Whilst public schools offered cadets, for less privileged children there were Sunday Schools and the Band of Hope - which tried to warn kids off the grog ('where there's drink there's evil!'). Free compulsory education was not provided by the State until after the 1870 Forster Act. By this time B.-P., now the 7th son, as three of Henrietta's children had died in infancy, had left Rose Hill preparatory school in Kent and joined Charterhouse school in London as a Gownboy. Known at home as Stephe or Steevie, one of his nicknames at Charterhouse was '**B**aking **P**owder'. He had no idea then that, well before meeting the Dutch settlers of South Africa, just around the corner from Charterhouse school was a thriving social and business community of Dutch settlers - the Dutch church is still there today. Indeed, one van Raalte (a name B.-P. would know well later as the owner of Brownsea Island) had a registered business at Charterhouse Buildings.

Left: Where B.-P. was born and first lived (right of ladder), 6 Stanhope Street (now 11 Stanhope Terrace). Remaining photos show B.-P.'s parents, Henrietta and The Rev. Professor Baden Powell.

B.-P.'s father would die when B.-P. was just 3

At her later home near Hyde Park, B.-P.'s mother kept bees in her drawing room. Situated next to a large organ, the two straw bee-hives had glass windows to allow visitors to watch the bees at work. A pipe connected the hives to an outside window.

Situated between the peaceful St. Paul's Cathedral on one side and the peculiar fragrances of Smithfields cattle market on the other, in 1870 we get a flavour (vegetarian!) of B.-P.'s early introduction to being under siege, this occurred whilst at school. An all too familiar pitched battle was taking place on the school's football ground between the Charterhouse boys and Smithfield's butchers' boys. During a game which the young B.-P. was watching, a hail of stones rained down on the ensuing fracas. The book *A History of Charterhouse* continues the story:

This was responded to from our side in like manner, with occasional sorties by strong bodies over the wall. Stephe was one of a small group of spectators too young to take part in the fray. Suddenly he was aware of his clerical headmaster standing next to him and saying:

'I think if you boys went through that door in the side wall, you might attack the cads in the flank.'

'Yes, Sir,' one of us replied, 'but the door is locked.'

The worthy doctor fumbled in his gown and said: 'That is so, but here is the key.'

And he sent us on our way rejoicing, and our attack was a complete success.

Two years later, with 117 boys, Charterhouse moved to new and greener pastures in Godalming, Surrey, where 37 new boys also joined them. Despite the austere conditions of large dorms, rats, deathly cold conditions in winter, and no flush toilets, young Powell (his name not yet hyphenated) made the most of it. Possibly he would have come under the eye of a truancy officer today as, when not sleeping or clowning in some lessons, he was out in the surrounding copse and woods practising his scouting. (Perhaps Charterhouse was the first school to try Scouting! although it wouldn't be until 1927 that they could officially record having a Scout Troop - started by Peter, B.-P.'s son.)

In fact, although not academically inclined, B.-P., the 'physical learner', was learning a lot of a practical nature. He said that it was through evading certain masters or lessons that he first honed his skills of observation, fire-lighting (without giveaway smoke signals), trapping animals and camp cooking.

Unlike some of the boys, B.-P. saw nothing wrong with the fagging system (it has echoes of his later using older boys as Patrol Leaders and role models for young Scouts to look up to). B.-P. was a useful goalkeeper whilst at Charterhouse, but the older boy he fagged for was Edward Parry, a much more skilful sportsman who went on to play in the 1880 FA Cup final and for England.

What was next? With his schooling finished it was time for a career, and this would be decided upon by his mother - now a widow who kept a firm hand on the family purse and her off-springs' upbringing. A military career was what she chose for B.-P. but not before he had spent time at Oxford - it was where his father had been, and where his older brothers Frank and George were doing very well.

He was scuppered! entrance to Balliol and, second choice Christ Church, was not to be. Charles Lutwidge Dodgson, the mathematics tutor (real name of Lewis Carroll, author of *Alice in Wonderland*) couldn't help but see the glaring truth: his mother, with the best of intentions, was the calculating social engineer, but calculations were beyond B.-P.

Through the traditional fagging system that existed at Oxford, strangely, Scouts were already in place - a scout was a gopher for older students. Several decades later the university would have real Rover Scouts, and even earlier, in 1909 undergraduates would help to run the local town Scout Troops - some of the earliest in the country. Perhaps there is also some poetic justice in B.-P. later receiving honorary degrees from Oxford, Cambridge and four other universities.

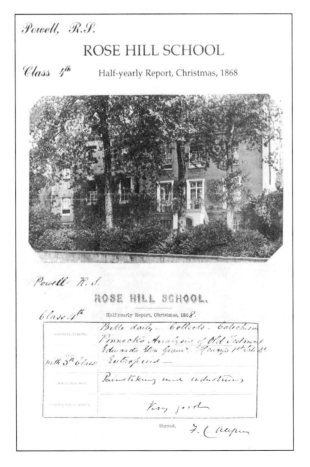

B.-P. aged 5, and
at Charterhouse

THE CHARTER HOUSE.

CHARTERHOUSE REPORT. *Christmas* 187~~3~~

R.S.S. *Baden Powell*
Fifth Form.
of 15 boys
Place 12

*3rd Set in the
Upper School.*

Remarks.

CLASSICS.

*θ. Seems to me to take very little interest
in his work. H.J. Evans*

MATHEMATICS.

10th in 19. Unsatisfactory. J. Moore

MODERN LANGUAGES.

French

Fair, — could behave better. BB.

NATURAL SCIENCE.

13th out of 15. Fair.

Charterhouse, Godalming 1872 and modern-day

Marks obtained by candidates for First Appointments to the Cavalry and Infantry, examined under the directions of the Civil Service Commissioners, 3rd July 1876

Number in Order of Merit	Number in Examination	Name	Mathematics	English Composition, Literature, and History	Latin	Greek	French	German	Experimental Sciences	Geography and Geology	Freehand (Drawing)	Geometrical (Drawing)	Total
		Maxima	3,000	1,600	3,000	2,000	2,000	1,600	3,000	2,000	1,000	800	—
1	277	Onslow; Richard Cranley	1,860	1,245	2,314	1,388	1,646				344	161	6,618
2	299	Wallace; Alexander	1,273	1,577			1,140	1,130				134	5,970
3	363	Hand; William Hudson		1,260			1,148	1,130				154	5,867
4	469	Widdicombe; William Sutherland		1,385			1,249					159	5,688
5	406	Harrisson; Cholmeley Edward Carl Bransfil	866	980	1,758	894	1,646					179	5,580
6	679	Baden-Powell; Robert Stephenson Smyth		850	1,762		1,365					147	5,530
7	700	Barter; Beamish St. John	950	1,346	1,453	886						341	5,280
8	159	Barkworth; Harold Arthur Sandbach	930	1,260	1,985	770	700					156	5,166
9	217	Lindsell; Philip Barber	898	1,205	2,042	715	680					110	5,066
10	297	Ringwood; Herbert	1,010	1,660	1,570		1,085					147	4,987
11	342	Sinclair; Clarence Granville		940	1,894		1,666				75	198	4,797
12	496	Walkstein; Francis Edward	964	1,295	2,203	1,187	978					134	4,727
13	491	Plummer; Herbert Charles Onslow		815			1,311	730				119	4,718
14	335	Bowring; George		1,865			789					147	4,657
15	189	Griffith; Thomas Llewelyn George		1,388			688					184	4,633
16	444	Mann; Frederick Henry		1,000	1,397							159	4,616
17	386	Davies; Thomas Arthur Harkness		530	1,614					570		186	4,467
18	695	Kitchener; Frederick Walker		1,705	2,301		913					150	4,407
19	396	Waterman; John Cecil de V.										159	4,406
20	441	Neele; Thomas Augustus	726	360	2,350				214			184	4,351
21	229	Justice; William Napier	980	1,029								184	4,337
22	423	Gethin; John Percy	1,366	545	2,319	822						151	4,231

A Career in the Army

The **seventh** month of 1876 would be a key moment in B.-P.'s life: in sitting entrance exams for a commission in the infantry and (to be safe) cavalry, B.-P. surprised himself by coming second in the cavalry list and fifth in the infantry out of a total of **718** men who sat both exams. One Herbert Plumer sat the same infantry exam on the same day; they would later become well acquainted. As a talented artist B.-P., if not the future Field Marshall Plumer, would have expected to have done well in the Freehand Drawing section. Oddly, out of a possible maximum 1000 marks (a peculiar marking system!) he scored just **75**.

And so it was on the **30th October** 1876, gazetted as a Sub-Lieutenant, that B.-P. left on the troopship *Serapis* bound for India. The **30th October** would prove to be a significant date. Not only was it the first time he had left British shores, he would later marry on 30th October and his first child, Peter, would be born a year later on the same date (two of the original Brownsea Island Boy Scouts were destined to die on **30th October** - 1914 and 1938).

Aboard the *Serapis*, the arduous five-week journey was almost unbearable for most of the crew. There were heavy seas, intolerable noise and heat on the lower decks, and even some children aboard who died. Nonetheless, in better moments B.-P. contributed well to the entertainments (whilst at Charterhouse B.-P. had gained popularity with his mimicry and acting skills). Indeed, he became something of an all-singing, all-dancing entertainer. He could sing (in falsetto if necessary), play the piano and ocarina, and dance. Aboard the *Serapis* he performed in *Cox and Box*, *Whitebait at Greenwich* and *Area Belle*. All this <u>and</u> being a talented artist. Able to draw equally well with either hand, he became a member of the London Sketch Club (then at 157 Bond Street).

It was also aboard the *Serapis* that B.-P. first met fellow officer George Noble. They became good friends and later his two sons would help to try out B.-P.'s boy scouting ideas at his experimental camp.

As a soldier abroad, B.-P. would spend around a quarter of a century in peaceful times and times of conflict in India, Afghanistan, Malta, Ireland, West and South Africa. As he would later tell his Scouts to do, he would not grouse during the hard times, instead he tried to make the most of every situation. It is also true to say that B.-P. was not a typical soldier. There has always been a slight irony in that the Scout movement has sometimes been accused, by a minority of critics, of being a military movement. Yet it has never been noted for its marching ability; instead, it is more noted for its camping and sing-songs around the campfire. B.-P., in the army and in the Scouts, always found formal parades and pomp and ceremony a turn-off. As a soldier, too, he was in his element when carrying out scouting duties. Either alone or with a partner, he would search for vantage points, the lay of the land, scouting the enemy using tracking skills. These excursions, often learnt from locals, also entailed navigation, finding water and local food sources - all part of his keen interest in bushcraft and backwoodsmanship.

Baden-Powell has been known to make mistakes! In his Scout writings he was all the more endearing for highlighting his own errors, this helped to reassure his young readers that it was ok to make a mistake. However, it was perhaps more unusual for a trained soldier to shoot himself in the leg. In his version, whilst in Afghanistan he was chasing a horse thief in the dead of night when the gun accidentally went off. Fellow officer George Noble recalled him as 'playing with his revolver'. (B.-P. could never have predicted that much later trouble in Afghanistan would lead to his handbook *Scouting for Boys* being blacklisted as a possible training manual/terrorist threat in 2004!)

Whether or not great at shooting, B.-P. became noted for his skill at pigsticking (a chance to hunt boars before the other type of Boer?). A somewhat risky and barbaric sport, the thrill of the chase is well described in B.-P.'s own book *Sport in War.*

Suddenly both horses fling round their heads, they are trembling in every limb with excitement. There he stands - not thirty yards from us - a grand grey boar with yellow curling tushes, and his cunning savage little eye glistening in the broad morning sunlight ... He swings round, trots for a few paces, and then breaks into a rough tumbling canter across the yellow grass ... Our horses are mad keen for the fray, and as one tears through the fresh cool air all bodily weight seems to leave one's extremities and to be concentrated into a great heartful of emotion.

The blood and gore of such sports would later be played down by B.-P. It might appear strange to some of us that he could at this time enjoy hunting and killing animals and yet he always had pets which he was devoted to. He certainly mellowed and discouraged boys from stealing birds' eggs, also writing that it was far better shooting animals with a camera than with a rifle.

Some of his enjoyment of pigsticking was in the riding and handling of horses. In polo he found equal pleasure and gained a high level of competence. This could not match that of his new officer companion 'the Boy' McLaren, who was a champion polo player. McLaren got his nickname through B.-P. taking him on first appearances to be aged about 14 when he was really around 20. They became inseparable and shared bungalow accommodation, calling it **B**loater **P**ark (McLaren would later assist B.-P. with his experimental boy scout camp. It would be another MacLaren who bought for the Boy Scouts Gilwell Park, their first proper training ground and campsite).

There is no doubt that, at the time, B.-P. liked the company of young men. It was a strength of his that he was very good company and was also keenly interested in the welfare and progress of his men, seeing and treating them as individuals. But there has never been any evidence that his relationship with McLaren or any of his male acquaintances was of a sexual nature. Although almost living as husband and wife at one stage, their relationship would not have been considered that out of the ordinary.

It was in the Ashanti Campaign (1895 - 96) that B.-P. - now a Brevet Lieutenant-Colonel - took command of an expedition to the Gold Coast in West Africa. This and other campaigns were messy and complicated affairs that involved corruption, distrust, greed and faults on all sides (the area would gain independence and become Ghana one hundred years after B.-P.'s birth, in 1957). B.-P. was part of the scheme to impose a **B**ritish **P**rotectorate and was involved in the fight and surrender of Prempeh, a ruler and king. It was in this terrain (also later in Matabeleland) that B.-P. adopted the use of a wooden staff, large handkerchief used as a cravat to protect against sunburn and dust, and a large broad-brimmed hat. Khaki clothing (khaki meaning dust-coloured in Urdu), along with the items above would all later be used as part of the Boy Scout's uniform. The big Stetson-style hat was often known as the **BP** hat (though BP really stood for the trade-name '**B**oss of the **P**lains'). It would become an icon in Britain and around the world for over half a century.

B.-P. was fortunate at this time to have some of his reports and sketches published in newspapers and journals, it earned him £170.00 and recognition. Even his brother was getting a mention in the *Daily Graphic* of February 1890 (in relation to the Western Australia Bill). B.-P., Arthur Pearson and John Hassall were all catching the public eye in 1890, unknowing that they would later meet and work together on a common project. Whilst brother George Baden-Powell was mentioned in the *Daily Graphic*, a photograph of B.-P. ('Colonel Baden-Powell of the 13th Hussars') also appeared in February, this time in *The Graphic* (page 197). Aspiring illustrator, *John Hassall, who would design the front covers of the *Scouting for Boys* fortnightly instalments, had his first sketch published in *The Graphic* in February 1890. Sir Arthur Pearson, who would become the Boy Scouts' principal sponsor and publisher, launched his enterprising *Pearson's Weekly* in 1890.

B.-P. went on to do active service in Matabeleland where, by this time, he had written two books that had scouting themes or content: *Reconnaissance and Scouting,* and *Cavalry Instruction*. But a third book would prove to lift him much higher in the public psyche. The final proofs of *Aids to Scouting for N.C.O.s and Men* were sent off in the last post to get out of the besieged town of Mafeking (as B.-P. had been completing his book, Rudyard Kipling - earning the name 'the new Dickens' - had been doing the same with his *Kim* - a story B.-P. would later use in *Scouting for Boys*). It was aids from journalists, in fact, that went a long way in publicising B.-P. the 'never say die' colonel, helping to make his latest army book hugely popular (it was also translated into German). For the defence of a once almost unknown little town called Mafeking, as it held out for **7** months against attack from the Boers, raised the **B**lood **P**ressure of the folk back home with trepidation and excitement from October 1899 to May 1900.

---

*Sadly, for John Hassall the relief of Mafeking would always be associated with the death of his first wife, who died whilst giving birth to their daughter. Funeral proceedings for Isabel Hassall were held during the 17th and 18th May 1900.

Close friend Major Wade stamps
some authority many years later!
(*Hampshire Herald* July 1957)

THE MAFEKING SIEGE
STAMPS

The True Story

So many loose and inaccurate statements have been made about these stamps that I determined to excavate the truth and clear B.-P. of a cruel libel.

The Boer War broke out on October 11th, 1899. On October 10th, 1899, B.-P.'s Chief Staff Officer issued the order: "The Boers talk of attacking Mafeking to-morrow afternoon. It is probable they will come in two or three columns from Rooigrond and Malmani, probably about five or six thousand strong, and surround the town."

This happened—and Mafeking was besieged from October 11th, 1899, to May 17th, 1900. During the siege, the Mafeking garrison ran out of supplies of all kinds, including postage stamps. So, the Commandant, Col. R. S. S. Baden-Powell, Commanding Frontier Force (I give him his official War Office rank and command which he then held), had to make good the shortage of postage stamps, which by law letters had to bear. The Postmaster at Mafeking, together with Major Lord Edward Cecil, designed without reference to B.-P. two stamps, one for 1d. and the other for 3d. The penny stamps bore a picture of Sergt.-Major Goodyear, of the Mafeking Boy Cadets, and the 3d. stamp bore a portrait—head and shoulders of B.-P. copied from a photograph taken in Bulawayo just before the siege.

It is this 3d. stamp that has caused all the bother, because it has always been the custom of the British Government (ever since 1840, when adhesive stamps were first used) for the head of the reigning sovereign to be on the stamps, and so, when B.-P.'s portrait appeared on them instead of the sovereign's, there was criticism, which has been repeated periodically ever since.

The difficulty was: there was no portrait of Her Majesty in the little frontier town of Mafeking that could be reproduced on the stamps and so as a mark of esteem to their gallant and most popular commander, B.-P., the Postmaster and the Chief Staff Officer therefore decided to use B.-P.'s portrait instead. I have a copy of this portrait and it is excellent.

When B.-P. was asked to approve of this design for the stamp he protested strongly, but by this time the stamps had been printed and were ready for sale, and eventually B.-P. approved, rather than make his overworked and half-starved staff do the work all over again.

When the stamps got to England rumour went round that the Queen was annoyed. That is all nonsense, because I have copies of her telegrams which she sent to B.-P. congratulating him on his remarkable skill shown in holding Mafeking for seven long, weary months and promoting him to be the youngest Major-General in the Army.

There is much more to all this than I can say at the moment as I have only just found all the necessary documents, but I have specimens of these siege stamps given to me by B.-P. and the Postmaster's original letter saying that he and Lord Edward Cecil put B.-P.'s head on them!

Major A. G. Wade, M.C.

The Siege of Mafeking

B.-P. had returned from another stint in India (Meerut) and was in London when, on the 7th July, Lord Wolseley issued instructions for B.-P. to come out to South Africa and raise a regiment of 590 irregulars (this was later changed to two regiments) in order to give a show of force. The grand plan included protection of Rhodesia, being a decoy to relieve other trouble spots, deterring natives from siding with the Boers, and preventing Boers from further uprising. It was not, at this time, his remit to travel to Mafeking and defend it. However, as events turned out, that's what he landed up doing.

Certain historians (later proved wrong) liked to think that B.-P. either wanted to be trapped in Mafeking so that he could engineer his own escape - all in a bid for personal fame and glory - or he foolishly allowed himself to become entrapped. More accurately, surrounded by an estimated 7000 Boers (experienced fighters with excellent local knowledge), and Mafeking being conspicuous by virtue of its geographically exposed position and not being a military post, these and other factors led B.-P. to carry out the only sensible decision possible: sit it out.

Approximately 870 miles from Cape Town, Mafeking ('Mafikeng' meaning 'the place of stones') was a small, unassuming town with 1,700 white and 5,000 black inhabitants. Despite historian Michael Rosenthal calling it 'a tin-roofed town with nothing particular to recommend it', Mafeking had become something of a liability as, beyond B.-P.'s control, more and more supplies had been stockpiled there. The locals, too, had asked for protection from the war-hungry Boers. All B.-P. had was a hastily gathered much smaller force, mostly untrained in shooting or riding, and with minimal armoury: four 7 pounder guns, two smaller calibre pieces and 7 .303 Maxim machine guns.

His skills of perseverance, calmness and thinking ahead during the siege would later be reflected in his Boy Scout handbook, where boys were urged to 'stick to it', smile and whistle through all difficulties, and **Be Prepared**.

Less than two decades later, with improved weaponry and the invention of the tank, the siege could only have lasted but a day or so. The whole Boer War, like others that followed, was confidently predicted to all be over by Christmas. In fact, it would be far longer, and the siege at Mafeking was not the first or last siege in the Boer War, though it did last for 217 days. With very little coming in or getting out, it became a game of cunning plans, a game of cat and mouse whilst they waited for the Boers to retreat or more forces to come to their aid.

Animals, being food, became an important topic of conversation. The horses, eventually and out of desperation, were completely recycled. The shoes were used in the manufacture of shells; its mane and tail were sent to the hospital and used for stuffing in pillows; its meat and insides were made into Mafeking sausages; the head and hide, once the hair was removed, were made into brawn; lastly, the bones were boiled up and made into soup (**Broth de Powell?**).

After receiving a note from a Boer emissary sent in under a white flag to persuade B.-P. to surrender 'to avoid further bloodshed', B.-P. listened with 'polite astonishment' and asked him to what bloodshed he referred, since to date only a chicken had died and a donkey been wounded. Similarly he wrote a communication to Colonel Plumer 'All well. Four hours' bombardment. One dog killed'. Although drafted differently by B.-P., this message got through to London and was picked up by the papers.

The wily colonel knew there were spies in Mafeking but he didn't know how many. Thus, on the **7**th October he erected a notice stating:

SPIES

There are in town today nine known spies.
They are hereby warned to leave before 12 noon
tomorrow or they will be apprehended.

IN 1900, A *TIMES* CORRESPONDENT DURING THE BOER WAR DESCRIBED B.-P. AS FOLLOWS:

Colonel Baden-Powell is young, as men go in the army, with a keen appreciation of the possibilities of his career. His countenance is keen, his stature short, his features sharp and smooth. He is eminently a man of determination, with great physical endurance and capacity, and extraordinary reticence. His reserve is unbending, and one would say that fever would be the only heat which would permeate his body. He does not go about freely, since he is tied to his office through the multitudinous cares of his command, and he is chiefly happy when he can snatch the time to escape upon one of those nocturnal, silent expeditions, which alone calm and assuage the perpetual excitement of his present existence. Outwardly, he maintains an impenetrable screen of self-control, observing with a cynical smile the foibles and caprices of those around him.

Actually, by the end of October he had arrested 28 suspected spies. And although he made light of situations and was a master of maintaining morale by organising competitions and entertainments (for example, the bonniest baby, or B.-P. becoming the flamboyant Paderewski - both sides had agreed to cease fire on Sundays), there were horrific deaths from shelling. These included children, as Tim Jeal reminds us:

A little white boy was playing with some marbles when was hit. Baden-Powell visited him in hospital the day he died. He was appalled by the terrible injuries he saw there: limbs missing, parts of faces and no adequate means of easing the victim's suffering. Mr Urry, the bank manager, avoided going near the hospital. 'The groans and shrieks of the dying are too terrible to hear.'

Despite the deaths and near starvation, ploys such as getting his men to step over imaginary barbed wire fences, and an 'array of powerful searchlights' constructed from one bodged biscuit-tin contraption hastily moved to different locations, all helped to frustrate the Boers' moves. An unexpected though ancient extra weapon was discovered being used as a gatepost; it was cleaned up and put into action. The ship's gun from Napoleon's time was discovered to have the initials **BP** on it (which actually stood for the foundry name of Baily and Pegg). They nicknamed it Lord Nelson (in fact, B.-P.'s mother always claimed she was a great-niece of Nelson's). This gun was a bonus, but the railway workshop had also constructed a 5-inch howitzer which had a superior range to the other guns in their armoury. It was known as the 'Wolf', a name that linked with B.-P.'s acquired name - Impeeza - from his time in Matabeleland. In the original *Scouting for Boys* there was a suggested Wolf badge to be awarded for exceptional Scouting work. The Wolf gun used in the Mafeking campaign can now be seen at the Royal Artillery Museum, Woolwich.

Although news of B.-P. and Mafeking was being followed with huge interest by Queen Victoria and the British public in the newspapers (particularly as there was scant good news elsewhere in the war), by April 1900 B.-P. had began to think about evacuating the town. He really felt that they couldn't hold out much longer. Fortunately, such plans never had to be implemented. What joy and surprise it was when eventually news of a relief column (squadron **617**) organised by Colonel Plumer (born the same year as B.-P., **1857**) arrived. And who should it be that first arrived to give Mafeking and B.-P. freedom? Baden Baden-Powell (there's a coincidence of names), he was B.-P.'s younger brother! (or so legend has it; he was certainly part of the relief column).

Fame and Foundations

News of the **British Pluck** of B.-P. and his men at the great siege, that had held out for **217** days and finished on the **17th** May, travelled over the cables from Pretoria and found its way to Reuter's offices in Old Jewry at 9.**17**pm. All over the country, and London in particular, there was wild celebration (not that there weren't critics of the South African War). B.-P.'s mother, now living at Hyde Park Gate, had to repeatedly come out on to her balcony and wave to the cheering fans. Children were given a day (or more) off school, and at Godalming, home of B.-P.'s former school, the vicar, fondly remembering B.-P.'s goal-keeping talent, raised a banner declaring *'Goal well kept, Baden-Powell.'* The new in-word of the day was 'mafficking', meaning - riotous rejoicing (used again in the 2nd WW). The **British Press** had a field day with reports on the 'principal actors' and the supporting cast; and new souvenirs were rushed out, including a **17** inch medallion.

An early indication of how B.-P. would become every boy's hero, and of how the Boy Scout idea gained currency can be seen in the *Boys of the Empire* magazine of 1900. A popular though rather  jingoistic boys' paper, the editor proudly announced on 27th October that B.-P.'s *Aids to Scouting* would be serialised. And so it was, as *The Boy Scout,* the term predating B.-P.'s eventual choice for his movement by seven years. The boys' serial, however, was largely a publicity ploy to increase the paper's **7000** or so young readership.

The 'conquering hero' did not return to England straight away, there were other engagements, and also the major task of setting up and training the South African Constabulary, whose role it would be to establish a pacification programme. The motto used by B.-P.'s SAC (and later the Boy Scouts) was **Be Prepared**. B.-P. also gained promotion to Major-General, the youngest officer to gain that rank. And an abundance of products continued to carry his name, including Baden-Powell cigars, dolls and board games. One young girl, Olave, went to her village shop and chose a button-hole badge of Baden-Powell rather than one of Lord Roberts or any of the other famous generals on offer. She would later become his wife.

Two chargers from the people of Australia were presented to B.-P. around this time, one was called Orara, the other **Black Prince** (prophetically standing for Olave and B.-P.). Black Prince was later used as a model for the illustrations in Anna Sewell's book *Black Beauty* (B.-P. would ride on him alongside the King at the Windsor Scout rally in 1911). Black Prince also featured as the Officer's Charger in the famous Royal Artillery painting *Forward the Guns* which was hung in the Royal Academy in 1917.

WELSH CONNECTIONS

In 1903 Major-General B.-P. returned to London to take up the duties of Inspector-General of Cavalry. Under the name of Colonel R Stephenson (to avoid interviews) he visited America to study American cavalry methods and tactics. Upon his return, amongst the many honours bestowed on him was the Freedom of Cardiff. His grandfather, Admiral Smyth, lived in Cardiff up to 1840, and had sole supervision of the Marquis of Bute's maritime and mineral properties in that locality. Admiral Smyth advised the second Marquis to construct the first dock in Cardiff - the West Dock - which was opened in October, 1839. Robert Stephenson, B.-P.'s God-father, was consulted by Lord Bute in connection with this and similar work. B.-P.'s mother also lived in Cardiff for a number of years.

After the formation of the Boy Scouts, the Prince of Wales (and future King), complete with big hat and shorts, became Chief Scout for Wales.

Much in demand: B.-P. (circled) at the opening of
the Salford Boys' Club, 1904 (still in existence today).

Back in England, on the **7th May 1903** B.-P., as Inspector of Cavalry, commenced his new job at the War Office. He had already been in demand in person and through correspondence with a wide range of boys' organisations, and this continued whilst he was in England. The Boys' Brigade had been founded in Scotland in 1883 (and would have a quarter of a century head start on the Boy Scouts), and in 1904 B.-P. was invited to inspect around **7000** boys and men of the Boys' Brigade at a parade held in Glasgow (he later became a Vice-President). Impressed as he was, he suggested that the marching and drilling side of the Boys' Brigade's programme would be well complemented and enhanced - attracting more boys - with some scouting games and activities. In part response, William Smith, founder of the Boys' Brigade, suggested that B.-P.'s popular army book *Aids to Scouting* (being used by boys and even some educational establishments) would be useful if it were rewritten for boys. B.-P. had a range of social and army commitments at this time, so a shortened, simplified extract was not written and published in the Boys' Brigade's *Gazette* until 1906 (with no great fanfare).

One tends to forget that both abroad and in England B.-P. met a wide circle of people - both famous and less well known - many of whom had an influence on him and his developing concept of scouting. The naturalist Ernest Thompson Seton was proving to be a popular author and illustrator of books on wildlife and folklore (Scott of the Antarctic, for example, took copies of his books on his expeditions). He sent B.-P. a copy of his new book about his Red Indian woodcraft scheme, where American boys were put into 'tribes' and practised woodlore/campcraft. B.-P. wrote later acknowledging Seton's useful ideas though stated that he wished to go ahead with his own scheme, but Seton would later unfairly accuse B.-P. of stealing his ideas. (B.-P. met Seton for the first time on **30th October** 1906.)

He was also a great fan of Buffalo Bill (Bill Cody). Billed as 'The Last of the Great Scouts' (and also as The **B**ayard of the **P**lains), B.-P. had first met him in 1887 and his scouting skills and colonial dress-sense of Stetson hat and scarf inspired him. He saw Cody again when he toured England with his numerous Wild West shows. B.-P. admired anything with cowboy-style flavour. It would also inspire others in the Legion of Frontiersmen, many of whose members assisted with Boy Scout training early on. So traditional and anti-modern life in some ways, in others B.-P. embraced new technology. He bought his first car in 1906. Buffalo Bill, incidentally, did not share B.-P.'s birthday (he was born four days after: 26th February, and died four days after B.-P.'s day and month of death: 12th January). Yet Cody's brother Samuel did share B.-P.'s birthday. Sadly, like B.-P.'s brother Augustus, who died young - at thirteen - Samuel would also die young, at twelve. His father also had a connection: he died in **1857**, the year of B.-P.'s birth.

The most significant meeting at this time, however, occurred in the **seventh** month of 1906 when B.-P. stayed at the Frensham home of millionaire publisher Sir Arthur Pearson. Owner of the *Daily Express*, in 1904 he had purchased the *Evening Standard* for £700,000.

Together it was agreed to promote the boy scouting idea and that B.-P. would draw up a scheme and new boys' handbook. With his army commitments not finishing for almost another year, Scouting's launch would still be on the back burner for some time.

And so it was that 1907 would prove to be the year that set things in motion. January saw publication of a short pamphlet on B.-P.'s suggested boy scouting scheme, followed later by another; these were sent to influential people. And with his army appointment at an end in May, B.-P., exactly 7 years after his Mafeking fame, still seemed to be in great demand (though in 1900 and years after he always played down the importance of his role in the success of the siege). For example, the *Sheffield Daily Telegraph* announced B.-P.'s visit to inspect the local Boys' Brigade and YMCA thus: 'Popular Hero in Sheffield'. Unknowing that a new boys' scouting movement was less than a year away from its launch, they unwittingly titled him the 'King of Scouts'. But also in that same month B.-P. managed to get away for a fishing trip in Ireland. It was here that he met the affable and wealthy Charles van Raalte, owner of Brownsea Island in Dorset (soon to be the **B**irth **P**lace of Scouting). But he needed to get his ideas down on paper first.

The van Raalte family, including grandparents.

A Book and an Island

In June 1907 B.-P. managed to complete a first draft of his handbook *Scouting for Boys* after staying briefly at the Walton Hotel in Dovedale, Derbyshire, then spending ten days at Mill House (featured below), a friend's residence situated close to the windmill on Wimbledon Common. Confusingly, Scout histories tend to show a photograph of the windmill (built in 1817) on the Common which, apart from its proximity to Mill House, had no connection to the house, B.-P. or his book. Since 1948 and still to this day there exists a plaque on the exterior of the windmill which states that B.-P. wrote parts of *Scouting for Boys* in Mill House in 1908. In fact the book was published in instalments from the 15th January 1908. B.-P. added most of the final touches while at Mill House in December, so it was virtually all completed in 1907.

Mill House came complete with a servant and menagerie of owls, marmosets, lemurs and penguins. Having got the scheme down on paper, would it work? Never mind the penguins, what B.-P. needed was guinea pigs. The **seventh** month of the **seventh** year would see B.-P. writing to friends and acquaintances, inviting them to send their sons on a holiday with a difference, to start at the end of July.

B.-P. nearly came to live on the Common. At a meeting of the Conservators of **30th October** 1911 it was recorded that Mrs. Fetherstonhaugh (a friend of B.-P.'s) had vacated Mill House. B.-P. was one of several applicants for tenancy. He was unsuccessful, as it went to a Mr Reeves on a **7** year lease at £100 p.a. rent.

WIMBLEDON CONNECTIONS

It is said that Brownsea Island was the birthplace of Scouting, but perhaps it could be argued that Wimbledon Common gives it a close run for its money. It was in Mill House on Wimbledon Common that B.-P. sat and worked away at his new Scouting handbook for boys. Wimbledon Common went on to host the first-ever district Scout competition. In May 1908 B.-P. was present to witness Scouts from south-west London and Hampstead districts compete in such tasks as fire-lighting and tent pitching.

The Common, once the site for duels, was the local home for members of the National Rifle Association. In 1874 B.-P. was part of a team which represented the Charterhouse cadets in the Ashburton Shield. They did not win though B.-P. was the only team member to score a 'bull'.

Strangely, during the Boer War there was a place called Wimbledon just outside Kimberley, the scene of another well known siege.

Publisher Sir Arthur Pearson, the movement's wealthy sponsor, went to school at Eagle House, Wimbledon. Much later, the Boy Scouts' first joint manager of 1908 (with Kenneth McLaren), Peter Keary, lived in Wimbledon.

B.-P.'s brother, Frank, once lived very close to the Common (he wrote a letter of complaint about the noise on the Common, some of which came from the raucous bugles belonging to the ubiquitous Baden-Powell Boy Scouts!).

Ralph Tubbs OBE, architect of Baden-Powell House (he also designed the Dome of Discovery for the 1951 Festival of Britain), was a resident of Wimbledon.

Some Wimbledon residents happen to have **BP** in their post-codes.

Right: Sir Arthur Pearson. By a quirk of fate his first published article in *Pearson's Weekly* was a piece on blindness; from 1908 his sight deteriorated to complete blindness.

In collaboration with the Marconi Company, Pearson was the first person to hold an appeal for funds (for the National Institute for the Blind) over the airwaves.

Brownsea, off Poole, is the largest of the 7 islands in that part of Dorset. Poole harbour is reputed to be the second largest natural harbour in the world. Today it is a bustling area of bobbing boats, shoppers and tourists. The Sandbanks area, where some of the boys - destined to become the world's first-ever Boy Scouts - left to go across to Brownsea, is said to have the 4th highest land prices in the world. Local home owners include footballer Jamie Redknapp, Elton John and Bruce Forsyth (the latter shares his birthday with B.-P.!).

Back in late July and early August of 1907, Poole was quieter and more parochial. Charles and Florence van Raalte were pleased to give B.-P. permission to run his 'boys' encampment' on their island, and proved to be pleasant and helpful hosts (they had a staff of around 70, including a professional golfer; they also possessed two steam launches). Coincidentally, before the van Raaltes' time on the island B.-P. had already been to Brownsea. As a boy, he and his brothers had sailed across from Poole harbour and landed on one of the Branksea (as it was then known) beaches. Young Olave, B.-P.'s future wife, too, had seen the island. Her father had a majestic home in **Branksome Park**, near Bournemouth, but Olave had moved with her family 17 times before they had settled in the nearby village of Lilliput (the author of *Gulliver's Travels* had lived there). This home was said to have splendid views across to Brownsea Island, so perhaps the future wife of Scouting's founder had espied the Boy Scout camp from afar.

In all there were 20 boys who camped on the island and took a full part in the eight days' programme; about half were from public schools and half from local Boys' Brigade companies (one, Ethelbert - 'Bert' - had the surname of Tarrant, several decades later another, soon-to-be-famous, Chris Tarrant became a Scout, apparently nicknamed Cuthbert in the Troop). These local boys had been selected by two local Boys' Brigade captains, Mr Green and Mr Robson. They both served B.-P. as quartermasters and, with good local contacts, were indispensable in getting supplies - particularly Mr Robson, who went on to own several provisions stores (though B.-P.'s request for a 'harpoon' - later used in a 'hunt the whale' boating game - was no doubt challenging for Robson and the local blacksmith!).

An engraving depicting a much earlier Brownsea

B.-P. and some of the boys going over to Brownsea

The actual campsite where it all started

The use of local town boys and public school boys was all part of B.-P.'s desire for a good social mix - quite a novel and daring idea then (though none of the boys were, as B.-P. and others later liked to say, poor lads, with some coming from the East End of London). Mafeking veteran 'the Boy' McLaren assisted B.-P., a cook was employed, and Donald Baden-Powell, B.-P.'s nine-year-old nephew, went as his uncle's adjutant and orderly. He would go on other Scout camps with B.-P. though later said that he didn't really enjoy his first Scout Camp!

The Camp was on a wilder part of the island than where the van Raaltes lived it up in their castle with numerous guests, including royalty from overseas (and not forgetting their pet monkey too).

Of course, the boys on that first camp weren't Boy Scouts proper, most of the boys just viewed it as a camping holiday with the famous colonel (actually a Lieutenant-General by this time); perhaps the equivalent of a group of boys today being selected to attend a camp with David Beckham, who had a new youth training idea he wanted to try out. Camping in 1907, it has to be remembered, was quite a novel idea. One of the boys, Terry Bonfield, had clear memories even eighty years after the camp:

We were taken by open lorry to Poole - all with our little kit bags. From Sandbanks we went across to the island and walked from the quay to the isolated camp. It was very exciting to a young boy - all very wonderful. We were given a groundsheet and two blankets and were told to use the kit bag as a pillow. We scooped out a little hole for our hips. I slept like a log.

The camp officially started on 1st August. The twenty boys were put into four patrols of five boys, with one of the boys being chosen as leader of his patrol. The patrols were named after birds and animals ~ Bulls, Wolves, Ravens and Curlews. Living and doing things as a patrol, and being put on their honour to always try their very best, would all become hallmarks of the Scout movement. It would single it out from other youth organisations, where the emphasis was normally on bigger group sizes, with the responsibility and leadership coming largely from the adults themselves (youth groups, corporate businesses and other institutions today who take their staff on team-building courses are often doing what B.-P. advocated back in 1907).

During the camp the boys learnt about such things as observation, life-saving, tracking, camping out, bridge and raft-making - all based on B.-P.'s ideas in *Scouting for Boys*. The yarns that would later appear in the handbook were entertaining but usually had a moral or teaching point to them. One of the former Brownsea boys, Humphrey Noble, could still recall in 1957 his awe in listening to B.-P. - his bullet-ridden Union Flag from Mafeking fluttering near his tent - tell of his many tales and exploits from foreign lands:

In the evening we gathered round the camp fire. There was no Summer Time then or Daylight Saving in those days so that it was dark at a reasonable hour, and B.-P. would tell us stories. He was a wonderful teller of tales and had had the most exciting adventures and escapes during his army life, culminating naturally in the famous Defence of Mafeking. He had a very clear resonant voice which arrested attention from the very first. So you can imagine us sitting there in the darkness round the fire listening spell-bound to some thrilling story.

Although the idea of the camp was to keep it all 'hush, hush' so that B.-P. could proceed with his experiment undisturbed (thus the location of a private island seemed ideal), local gossip would have been rife; also, the local paper had briefly announced the famous General's forthcoming 'boys' encampment'. Pearson, the great entrepreneur and sponsor, unsurprisingly, had a paragraph on the camp in his *Daily Express* whilst the camp was actually in progress (see below). When the question is asked, 'Who founded the Scout Movement?', one is tempted to say that Pearson was the cofounder.

BOY SCOUTS IN CAMP.

"TREASURE ISLAND" IN BOURNEMOUTH BAY.

THE DAY'S WORK.

"Express" Special Correspondent.

POOLE, Wednesday Night.

Visitors to Bournemouth know well by sight the little island known as Branksea, lying in the almost landlocked bay at the head of which is this ancient port; but the foot of the ordinary tourist is not often set on this romantic island, which is at present the happy hunting ground of General Baden-Powell and his corps of boy scouts.

The island is the property of Mr. Van Raalte, who has a lovely old castle at the seaward end, looking across to the long line of great sandhills that form the western extremity of Bournemouth.

A few cottages at the little island's harbour, a few more at the northern end, looking across the water to Poole, and a few scattered keepers' lodges constitute the permanent abodes on the island, which is about a mile and a half long and rather less across.

This afternoon I ran down the bay in a motor-boat from Poole to the castle, and then I set out on foot to track the scouts to their lair.

"TRACKLESS" FORESTS.

The greater part of the island is covered with forests of pine and beech trees, with thick undergrowth and sand tracks. The woods were so dense and the air was so still, save for the chirping of innumerable birds and the quacking of wild duck on little meres, that I thought for a time that I had discovered "Treasure Island" anew.

At last I saw a kind of "Spyglass Hill," with a few pines at the top, and when I had climbed it I saw, down by the shore below, the little all-alone camp of the scouts. There was one large tent—the mess tent—flanked by two smaller ones. These two are the sleeping places of the General and of Major Maclaren, an old fellow-soldier who is helping him to train the scouts. As I reached the little camp I spied a tall, thin man, bareheaded, with his jacket and waistcoat off, disappearing over the further hillside. I anticipated what I heard—that it was "B.-P." off on the trail by himself.

There were about a dozen scouts in camp this afternoon, and the rest were due to-night. There will be twenty in all. Those who had arrived were putting up their own tents under the major's directions, and when they had finished the job they fetched trusses of hay, on which, covered with a waterproof, they will sleep.

NO DIVISIONS OF RANK.

Some of them are Eton and Harrow lads, some belong to boys' brigades, but all boys are boys when General Baden-Powell has the handling of them, and there are no artificial divisions of rank. The little camp promises to be one of the most delightful memories of these youngsters, for the hero of Mafeking intends teaching them how to follow the trail, how to find a few grains of Indian corn in an acre of heather, and how to hide and discover messages in trees and under stones.

From six in the morning until 9.30 at night there will be scouting, and scouting intermixed with bathing and feeding on plain fare.

Every night an hour will be spent round the "camp fire," and the boy scouts will hear some of the best tales about Mafeking ever told.

B.-P. stuck in the bog! Arthur Broomfield, a local lad who'd spent most of his life on the island, watched wistfully from afar the camp proceedings. Fortunately, in 1957 he also provided the movement with a unique account of the Camp in *The Scouter* magazine:

By 1907 most of my brothers and sisters had grown up and left the island. I was the only one still at school. It was during the long summer holiday that Baden-Powell arrived, and so I had plenty of spare time in which to follow closely all that happened. My father told me to keep away from the camp unless I was invited to go there, so for a while I had to be content to look on from a distance. Every day I went to a vantage point a few hundred yards from the camp and watched the busy preparations ...

Sometimes I would row slowly along close inshore to get a better view. This eventually led to my being hailed by some of the boys, and I invited them to come out for a pull in the dinghy. Gradually I made friends with them, and I began to take part in their Scouting activities. Tracking and woodcraft were already second nature to me, and I knew every plant, animal and bird on my island home.

Then came the memorable meeting with Baden-Powell himself. The founder of the Scout Movement had been my hero for many years. I never tired of reading about his many exploits in Africa and other lands. The siege and relief of Mafeking was one of my earliest memories of outstanding events in the Boer War. I remember, too, the Baden-Powell mug which I carried home so proudly. You can imagine the thrill I felt when I met my hero face to face.

One evening in August I was walking along the path that led from my home to the camp. It was very hot. Nightjars were burring away in the trees, and the mosquitoes were humming around in clouds as I scuffed my way along a path carpeted with slippery pine needles. Bracken grew waist-high on either side. On my right rose the pine-clad hillside, and on my left the heather and gorse-covered ground sloped down to the sea.

I had reached the point where the camp came into sight when I heard someone calling me. I looked down the hill and saw a man floundering in a patch of bog. There were many such patches near the camp, where one might sink knee-deep in soft rust-coloured mud.

I ran across the rough ground and showed the stranger the way out of the bog. As he came towards me I realised that he was none other than Baden-Powell himself. I was too overwhelmed to speak audibly as he clasped my hand, and asked my name and where I lived. I grabbed a handful of bracken, and wiped the mud from his shoes and stockings. The great man smiled down at me, patted my shoulder and thanked me for helping him. Then, proud and excited, I ran home to tell my parents about my adventure.

After that I saw Baden-Powell again several times, when I was invited to join the Scouts round their camp fire, and I listened with rapt attention to his stories.

The Camp came to a triumphant close on the last day with a special show put on by the boys themselves. The van Raaltes and their guests, along with some of the boys' parents and islanders, watched as the newly trained Boy Scouts took part in competitions and demonstrated their newly acquired skills. Author Bill Hillcourt describes the 'proof of the pudding' final scene:

It ended in a tug-of-war between the 'birds' (the Curlews and the Ravens) and the 'beasts' (the Wolves and the Bulls), won by the 'birds'. Time and again the audience broke into appreciative applause. And when the show was over, the van Raaltes invited the whole camp to Brownsea Castle for a banquet-like tea in the beautiful dining-room, with a brass band from Poole playing on the terrace outside. At the call of one of their number, the boys gave three cheers for the 'best General in the world' and three more for their hosts, then returned to their tents and to the sad task of beginning to strike camp.

B.-P. supervising
a tug-of-war

Making mats

Right: The Commemorative stone by Don Potter, a one-time Cub, Scout and carver at Gilwell Park. The stone was unveiled by the B.-P.s' youngest daughter, Betty, in 1967. Potter went on to teach art at Bryanston School, Dorset (the present Lord Baden-Powell is a former pupil).

This Stone Commemorates the experimental Camp of 20 boys held on this site from the 9th August 1907 by Robert Baden-Powell later Lord Baden-Powell of Gilwell, Founder of the Scout and Guide Movement

BELIEVE IT OR NOT. . .

Like the B.-P.s (later on), the van Raaltes had a son and two daughters (as did Sir Arthur Pearson and Rudyard Kipling, also John Hassall in his first marriage). In 1906 the van Raaltes' son, Noel, gave a good pre-Scouting example of citizenship and helping others by rescuing a man drowning in Poole harbour (his name was J.R. **Poole**). Fifteen-year-old Noel received a Diploma from the Royal Humane Society for his act of bravery. Noel went on to marry three times. He had a passion for building/racing motor-boats, and later settled in Hamble, close to the first Sea Scout camp organised by B.-P. Noel died in 1936, aged 50, the same age as when his father would die in late 1907.

After Florence van Raalte sold the island in 1927, its new owner, Mrs. Mary **Florence** Bonham Christie, became reclusive and would not allow Scouts or anyone else to visit the island as she wanted to turn it all back to nature (locals called it the 'Forbidden Island'). The conveyance of Brownsea to Mrs. Bonham Christie in 1927 was to 'Charterhouse Investment Trust Ltd'. The church on the island is St. Mary's (though was not named after Mary Bonham Christie).

Close neighbours to the Baden-Powell family when B.-P. was born were the Christies, who also lived in Stanhope Street. Brook Street adjoined Stanhope Street, and Brook Street was one of the London homes of the van Raaltes (actually it was a second Brook Street in London but not very far away).

All of Mrs. Bonham Christie's estates were situated on the edge of oil fields: Addington Park, near Tunbridge Wells; Marston, near Frome; and Brownsea Island.

Mrs. Bonham Christie's son shared B.-P.'s first name, Robert. Her grandson, John (a former Scout) allowed fifty Scouts to visit the island in 1961.

There is a **BP** island next door to Brownsea! Furzey, the neighbouring island, is occupied by BP Plc and used for oil research and drilling.

The Unstoppable Train!

After the camp, which had been a great success, the boys went their separate ways. Immediately after the parts of *Scouting for Boys* were published fortnightly from January 1908, B.-P. and the newly opened Scout office in London started to receive hundreds of enthusiastic letters from boys and adults interested in the scheme. Sadly, by this time Charles van Raalte, hugely liked and respected locally, had died whilst in India. Perhaps not so surprisingly to most readers by now - he was born in that familiar year: **1857**. In October of 1907 he and his wife had started a long overseas holiday. In what turned out to be his last letter, sent as he left Egypt and headed towards Calcutta, he joyfully recorded the coincidence of him being in Egypt some twenty years before, on his honeymoon. Sadly, he quickly became very ill in India and died of pneumonia (his body was eventually returned to Brownsea and a private family funeral was held in the island church).

Boys across Britain purchased the fortnightly parts of B.-P.'s book and read through the 70 or so pages avidly. Although the book appeared somewhat peculiar to most adults - it was on cheap paper and seemed a mishmash of ideas - many of them were also intrigued with the famous soldier's latest work that had been put on the shelves of W H Smiths at railway stations and elsewhere. Some decided to purchase the novel 'self-help' book for boys and mentors.

Whilst some members of the YMCA and other boys' organisations decided to adopt or adapt B.-P.'s scheme, boys of their own accord also tracked down clergymen, schoolmasters, uncles, anyone they could think of to become their Scoutmaster. For once, B.-P. would find himself totally unprepared for what was happening! Independent Scout Patrols sprang up and grew into Troops, local Troops grew into local Scout Associations... Few were aware of it at the time, but the same thing was happening in many other places in Britain and around the world. (In fact, in 1910 the 1st Mafeking Scout Troop was founded; it remained in continuous existence until the most recent of years.)

Scouting for Boys was published as a complete handbook in May 1908, and a weekly Scout's paper, *The Scout,* had already been launched the previous month (B.-P. would earn around £750 in the early years in royalties from *Scouting for Boys* though he gifted the copyright to the BSA). In modern parlance it was manic during the first year or so; really, organised chaos as supply could not keep up with demand. The book itself had **7** impressions within the first two years and went on to become a best seller. Pearsons had let the BSA have the use of some rooms in Covent Garden (with an apposite address: Goschen Buildings, in Henrietta Street - B.-P.'s mother was called Henrietta, and Goschen was a region in South Africa), but the Scout 'office' could hardly cope with the demand for badges and enrolment cards (not to mention complaints - occasionally about undesirable Scoutmasters or from irate landowners annoyed with 'marauding Boy Scouts').

B.-P. himself was not in a position to commit much time to the 'monster' he'd created (a likeable one if there is such a thing) as, until 1910, he was in the north of England undertaking his duties as Commander of the Northumbrian Division of the Territorials. His movement, by this time, had exceeded 107,000 members (the actual Boy Scout membership seemed to coincide with the first two digits of the years they represented: 1910 ~ 100298 Boy Scouts; 1911 ~ 113909; 1912 ~ 126431; 1913 ~ 137776). It had taken the Boys' Brigade over twenty years to achieve a membership of around 63,126 boys; yet in 1913 the Scout movement dwarfed all other youth organisations with 137,776 Scouts (on the other hand, even in this early period the USA had far more Boy Scouts than the founding country).

The strangeness of the newly outfitted boys in the first decade of a new century, and the seepage of the Boy Scouts into almost every facet of life is perhaps rather forgotten or underestimated today. It all happened so quickly and often spontaneously. The left-hand shake, the special way a Boy Scout was supposed to tie his laces, the call signs and insignia: seemingly overnight boys were captivated by the scheme and, happily for many mothers and school teachers, turned into a new breed of boy. Author H. G. Wells wrote at the time (in *The New Machiavelli*, 1911):

There suddenly appeared in my world - I saw them first, I think, in 1908 - a new sort of little boy - a most agreeable development of the slouching, cunning, cigarette-smoking, town-bred youngster; a small boy in khaki hat, and with bare knees and athletic bearing, earnestly engaged in wholesome and invigorating games up to and occasionally a little beyond his strength - the Boy Scout. I liked the Boy Scout.

Some of the Boy Scouts' persona and helpfulness of the past makes good comedy material today, yet one too easily forgets that there were no road crossings or driving tests in the movement's earliest decades, traffic came from all directions. The new motor car was a fast and frightening prospect to many (the ubiquitous horse traffic, on the other hand, just as potentially lethal when panicked). In a time before the telephone was commonplace, being able to send signals, read maps or deliver urgent messages was of value. Of even greater value (before the NHS, ambulance service and professional fire brigades) was a knowledge of first-aid and rescue from gas, fire or floods. Being taught to cook or, for the Jobman badge, how to fit panes of glass and hang paper, gave boys life skills they didn't get in school. Additionally, B.-P.'s dictum that every Boy Scout should do a daily good-turn proved a huge public relations success. Soon, their sheer numbers and frequent outdoor activities, too, meant that they had an automatic high profile and were often on hand to help put out a fire or help a damsel in distress.

The brief 'impact list' (1908 - 1914) on page 42 only hints at the bonanza impact the movement had on society from its earliest of years. The movement became, in little more than a decade, a world-wide movement with several million registered members (there were many unregistered Scout Troops too, and Scouting was often also being done by the various other boys' organisations).

The high profile of the Boy Scouts, of course, meant there were advantages on both sides. People generally liked what they (Scoutmasters) were doing - occupying boys and training them in a constructive though fun way - so were supportive and encouraging. For example, a Scout's uniform could earn him reduced rates at the swimming pool; local doctors and the fire brigade would help with instruction. But the Boy Scouts were also good for business: photographic studios, hauliers, refreshment rooms, clothing manufacturers and suppliers, stationers, food suppliers when at camp - these and many others benefited.

A down side would be that some critics from within the movement and from some outside accused the Scouts of being too commercial and showy. This was not helped by Pearson's publishing reputation (though other publishing firms were doing similar things). A 'follow-up camp' in the summer of 1908, for example, had been publicised as a competition for boys to camp with B.-P. The Humshaugh camp, held on the Northumbrian Moors, had been run through the newly launched *The Scout*, where boys had to collect as many coupons as possible in order to secure a place (so needed money to buy as many copies as possible!).

The firm Merryweather donated a new fire-fighting appliance to the Boy Scouts Association, it is seen here being unlimbered in Victoria Street.

Eventually things got on a sounder footing: a move to independent offices in Victoria Street, a rule book was published and proper registration systems and local committees were set up. In addition to influential people heading the newly established committees, the movement attracted several famous patrons too. In addition to royal patronage, B.-P.'s brother Baden was a president (he inspected 700 Scouts at the Hurlingham Club in 1912, for example), but Lord Kitchener, Sir Ernest Shackleton and Sir Arthur Conan Doyle were also leading members of local Scout committees. Well known cartoonist Bernard Partridge (it's those initials again) would produce, for *Punch* magazine, the movement's first of many media cartoons (see the example below).

OUR YOUNGEST LINE OF DEFENCE.

Boy Scout (to Mrs. Britannia). "FEAR NOT, GRAN'MA; NO DANGER CAN BEFALL YOU NOW. REMEMBER, *I* AM WITH YOU!"

The Boy Scout: trusty and loyal

SCOUTING'S EARLY IMPACT ON SOCIETY

In early 1908 *Scouting for Boys* was reviewed in the local and national press. Throughout the year Boy Scouts hit the media with countless reports and photographs in local and national publications. A silent film *Scouts to the Rescue* was released.

Boy Scouts cropped up in every conceivable publication imaginable, many with no previously known link with boys or youth work (examples: the *Jewish Chronicle* and *Flight*).

In 1909 the first of numerous Boy Scout cartoons appeared in *Punch*. Baden-Powell received a knighthood from Edward V11.

The first national Boy Scout Rally was held at the Crystal Palace, 1909. 11,000 Scouts present; the King sent a telegram and personally inspected Scouts at a rally in Norwich the following month. Glasgow then followed with a large rally.

In 1910 Scouts took part in the Military Tournament at Olympia. In the same year two Boy Scout Patrols were taken with B.-P. to tour Canada.

In 1911 33,000 Scouts were present when the new King reviewed King's Scouts at a rally in Windsor Great Park. Also in 1910/11 the *Daily Telegraph* launched an appeal fund on behalf of the Boy Scouts. In the same year the Oxford English Dictionary included a new entry: 'Boy Scout'.

In 1912 the Boy Scouts were incorporated under Royal Charter. Chappells published a Boy Scouts' Marching Song; Gamages department store sponsored a Scouts' shooting shield; Sea Scouts appeared in the Lord Mayor's Show. By this time a Boy Scout had appeared in the fiction of Wodehouse and H. G. Wells, and also in a West End play; Kipling wrote a Patrol song for Scouts in 1909 (and *Land and Sea Tales for Scouts and Guides* in 1923).

In 1913 the King appointed the Duke of Connaught as the Boy Scouts' President.

In 1914 the Marconi company ran a competition for youth organisations. The winning Scout Troop was presented with a Field Station Wireless Apparatus.

Leslie Paul, who as a young man joined/led breakaway youth movements, still had fond memories of his time in the Scouts. In *Angry Young Man* he wrote:

Presently, of course, I yearned to play in the band, and as a Wolf Cub I stepped along whistling away at my fife, and later graduated, as a Boy Scout, to a side drum. Nothing I did elsewhere, in school or in church, ever brought me the same pride as my achievements in Scouting. It was the only social organisation interested in taking me into the country, and through it I made long forays, running and walking, as part of a trek-cart team which ranged far and wide through Kentish lanes. We spent days by the Ravensbourne, cooking, learning to light fires, swimming and playing games...

Left: A little remembered appearance of B.-P. again on Wimbledon Common, May 1908. He watched as Hampstead Scouts competed with local Scouts in lighting fires, pitching tents and other activities.

Right and below: Around 1908 the AA deployed 'scouts' to warn their hasty members of lurking policemen.

Sympathetic (?) Boy Scouts from Sandroyd School

A Boy Scout parade of 1909, Princes Street, Edinburgh.

The Movement's Early Years

It was in 1909 that the movement held its first national rally and public demonstration (the first of many) at the Crystal Palace in south London. It happened to be almost on the birthday of B.-P.'s mother - the 3rd of September - the rally was on the 4th. It was the first major opportunity for Scout Troops from all over the country to see what each other was doing. The King even sent a telegram to be read out. As the Scouts' Promise contained the phrase 'I will do my best to do my duty to God and to the King', which was something no other youth organisation included at the time, it forged a strong bond with one of, if not the,

most influential families in the land, with benefits for both parties. The King soon encouraged the addition of a new badge, the King's Scout Award. The Church, on the other hand, would always be ultra quick to remind the movement about its duty to God. From its inception and right across the decades, the relationship between some members of the Church and some members of the movement has ranged from disastrous, disputatious, cordial through to excellent.

Right from 1908 through to the 1920s B.-P. found himself dealing with staffing factions and disputes, and the expansion of a movement that seemed to be galloping away from him. Disputes and splits were inevitable (just about every youth organisation has had its breakaway branches); old Carthusian Sir Francis Vane would be the first leading figure to split (reluctantly) from B.-P.'s movement and help the new breakaway British Boy Scouts. When it wasn't about compatibility, it would be politics and religion that reared their heads. Certain Church members weren't happy 'to mix' with others, some found the movement not pacifist enough, and in Ireland there was a problem with the oath - one branch being loyal to B.-P. but not prepared to swear allegiance to the King.

But such problems were small in comparison to the snowball craze bursting through each new year. 1910 and 1911 would see B.-P.'s movement, yet again, land on its feet; B.-P. was also able to devote most of his time to the movement after retiring from the army on the 7th May 1910. The *Daily Telegraph* had raised over £7000 in an appeal fund for the movement; additionally, by 1911 a farm had been given to the Scouts. Called **B**uckhurst **P**lace, for boys over 15, it gave proper training to the resident Scouts in all aspects of farming. At this time and for several decades, the Scouts did a lot in preparing boys for work. A Scoutmaster's reference carried a lot of weight; local committees even set up juvenile labour exchanges for Scouts in times of high unemployment (no doubt some parents were shrewd enough to push their boys into the Scouts regardless of their own opinions over religion, class or militarism).

For B.-P. and the movement, the following year would prove to be one of extreme emotions. By this time the Girl Guides had been well established with the help of Agnes, B.-P.'s sister (whilst the inventor Guglielmo Marconi, an acquaintance of B.-P.'s, had been carrying out some of his radio communication experiments near Brownsea, he'd also been communicating his feelings towards Agnes - they had a brief courtship). Despite the fear that offering girls the chance to do Scouting would raise a generation of coarse girls with hairy lips, the girls who replaced their Scout hats for more feminine ones, and occupied the Elves and Pixie Patrols instead of the Lions and Cobras, pacified most protestors. Until a special handbook was produced the girls used *Scouting for Boys*. They did, however, have regular pages in a Pearson magazine called *Home Notes* (this had been registered as a women's magazine on **22nd February** 1894; it later became *Woman's Own*. Strangely, there had even been a Scout magazine long before the movement began: *The Scout,* a Socialist magazine, was published in 1895).

It was in January 1912 that B.-P. boarded the RSS *Arcadian* (Robert Stephenson Smyth?), she was on her maiden voyage and he was bound for America as part of a world tour to promote the movement. It had been the visit of W. D. Boyce - a wealthy publisher from Chicago - to London that had inspired him, on his return to the States, to start Boy Scouting there (this has echoes of Pearson, the wealthy publisher, promoting Scouting in Britain). Boyce, in London preparing for his ballooning and hunting adventures in Africa, had lost his way in a London fog, only to be led to his intended address by a Boy Scout who, doing his good-turn, refused any payment. Boyce would also later launch his unique Lone Scouts scheme for newspaper boys out in the sticks (it happened to be launched on the same day as B.-P.'s wedding anniversary - **30th October**). Famous former Lone Scouts include Burl Ives and Douglas Fairbanks.

Strangely, whilst on the *Arcadian* and bound for America, the USA President at that time (the 27th) was William Taft, born in **1857**. B.-P. would meet him along with other eminent Americans at the White House (**7** years later the Scouts would have their own White House at Gilwell Park!). Taft became Honorary President of the BSA (not the Boy Scouts Association but the Boy Scouts of America). Bizarrely, America's first president, George Washington, shares a familiar birthday - **22nd February 17**32. Had B.-P. opted to delay his tour by a few months he might have ended up on the *Titanic* - possibly leading to a very different history of the Scout movement. W. D. Boyce's daughter, incidentally, was called Happy. Perhaps she was not entirely happy with local gossip surrounding her husband. He'd survived the *Titanic* disaster but it was widely rumoured that he had dressed up as a woman in order to get an early place on a lifeboat.

Scouting for a Wedding

B.-P. would travel more than 70,000 miles on his tour and would also hear news that the Boy Scouts' Royal Charter had come through. Among the eminent passengers aboard the *Arcadian* was Dr. Treves. A Dorset man, Treves was from the London Hospital, was a founder of the British Red Cross Society and well known for treating the 'Elephant Man' (he had also served in the Boer War). But an unknown young lady was lying in wait to capture the famous soldier! Cruising with her father, Harold Soames, despite the age-gap both Olave Soames and B.-P. fell head over heels in love. She'd initially written in her diary: *'There is only one interesting person on board and that is the Boy Scout man.'* As per his book *Reconnaissance and Scouting,* furtive sorties were undertaken, secret rendezvous made and notes secreted in the cleats of the covered lifeboats (a romance blossomed rather like the one depicted in the *Titanic* film of 1987, only this was for real). By the 17th of January Olave's feelings were much stronger and more intimate in her diary:

Up before dawn just to see him and kiss him. See Venezuela coast in distance ... Small talks with various people and the beloved Scout is always there. He gives me a photo album and sketches ... I adore him.

And yet their meeting might never have happened. When Olave's father had first tried to book berths for the cruise he was told he was too late. They only got tickets at the last moment, after two cancellations came through.

Strangely, B.-P. had seen, or, rather, observed (though not met) Olave before. On first meeting her on board the *Arcadian* he asked Olave if she lived in London, and was puzzled to find that she did not. He continues in his autobiography:

Wrong. My sleuthing was at fault; she lived in Dorsetshire!
'But you have a brown and white spaniel?'
'Yes.' (Surprise registered.)
'Were you never in London? Near Knightsbridge barracks?'
'Yes, two years ago.'

Amazingly B.-P. had put his skill in observing different types of gait into practice. He recalled seeing this young lady walking with a purposeful stride in Hyde Park with her dog in 1909. He would also find out that she shared his birthday: **22nd February**.

The wide age-gap - she was 23 and he 55 - would not have been as surprising as today (although he was actually slightly older than Olave's father); in fact, B.-P.'s father's marriage to Henrietta had seen a similar age-gap. They would marry quietly in St. Peter's Church, Parkstone, near Brownsea (B.-P. forgot his razor and was loaned one by a butler!). The *Arcadian* would later be torpedoed in 1917 with the loss of 277 lives, but a much bigger sea tragedy for the Scout movement would occur on home waters and before B.-P. had returned to England for his wedding.

KEEPING IT IN THE FAMILY

Olave's sister, Auriol, also married a Robert (the previous year after meeting aboard a cruise ship): at the same church, same vicar, and in the same month.

Just as her parents and aunty had done, Olave and B.-P.'s daughter, Betty, would meet her future husband whilst on a cruise ship.

Betty was born in 1917, her husband, Gervas Clay (middle name Robert!), in 1907. Like B.-P. he had also played in goal for Charterhouse. Like Betty's parents, Gervas and Betty shared the same birthday - 16th April. Their son Robin was born on the 16th April. Later, a grand-daughter, Olivia Baden-Clay, was born on Auriol's birthday.

Heather, the B.-P.s' first daughter, had two sons. Michael was born on Auriol's (Olave's sister's) birthday; Timothy was born on his grandparents' birthday.

If the B.-P. weddings and birthdays seem purely chance, I might add that Peter, B.-P.'s son, also followed the family tradition and married Carine Boardman, who shared his birthday.

Olave's brother was Arthur Soames. His son Christopher (Olave's nephew) married Sir Winston Churchill's daughter, Mary. Their son Nicholas Soames is the Conservative MP for Mid-Sussex.

Rudyard Kipling's family (Kipling was a near neighbour of the B.-P.s') also had a tendency for coincidental dates: Charles van Raalte had died on 31st December, Kipling's wife was born on 31st December. Kipling was born on 30th December and their first child was born almost on their birthdays - 29th December.

Right: B.-P. and Olave at the Soames' family home.

Tragedy Strikes

The movement's first major accident involved the loss of life for eight south London Boy Scouts from the 2nd Walworth Scout Troop on 4th August 1912. The Troop was founded by former Dulwich College pupil Sydney Marsh, a City worker who enjoyed living and working among the poor of Walworth. They were sailing down the Thames and on in to the estuary when their ex-naval cutter, arriving close to Leysdown, site of their intended summer camp, came upon a dramatic change in weather and sea conditions which resulted in the boat capsizing and 8 of the 25 boys drowning (including one with the name **Baden Powell**). One of the survivors, Edward Beckham, is related to England footballer David Beckham. It became a national disaster, with the *Daily Chronicle* describing the funeral and procession from St. John's Church to Nunhead cemetery:

No other episode, not even a Royal procession, has brought so many people into the street or kept them there during a thunderstorm and deluge of rain. The crowds were so immense, that the mounted police at the head of the funeral procession had no small difficulty in forcing a way through them.

A *Daily Express* memorial fund was set up which resulted in the erection of a fine bronze Boy Scout statue. It was designed by Sir Giles Gilbert Scott, designer of Liverpool Anglican Cathedral and also, in 1927, the red GPO telephone box. Coincidentally, he was the architect of Charterhouse School's War Memorial Chapel (the largest in Britain). Additionally, the Walworth boys had started their river trip from Waterloo Bridge; Scott designed the new Waterloo Bridge.

The 2nd Walworth Boy Scouts with Scoutmaster
Sydney Marsh, practising on the Thames.

Left: Funeral proceedings outside St. John's Church

Right: The original memorial by Sir Giles Gilbert Scott, RA

Below: The modern replacement

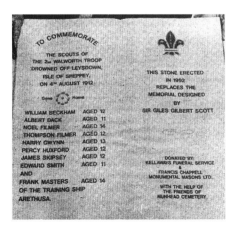

Sadly, the memorial, a local landmark along Scouts' Path in the cemetery, although surviving two World Wars was vandalised in the late 1960s by being hacked off at the ankles and stolen (possibly for scrap metal). It had been worth c£450 when it was completed in 1914 - the price of a substantial house then - and was only worth c£45.00 scrap in 1969. It was not until 1992 that a new memorial tablet was erected in the cemetery. A little later, in 1997, the original bronze plaque that had been attached to Gilbert Scott's Boy Scout statue turned up in the yard of a south London scrap metal dealer. It is now in the hands of the Scout Association. A replica of the original plaque was made and presented to Nunhead cemetery by Robert Stephenson (two of B.-P.'s names!) of Brompton cemetery.

SOME MORE COINCIDENCES....

Baden-Powell had preached at St. John's Church, Walworth (the boys' local church and sponsor) long before the start of the Scout movement. Not **the** Baden-Powell, but a Rev. J. Baden Powell, whose visit was reported by the *South London Press* in July 1882 - he was from the founder's family. Charlie Chaplin, incidentally, was a local lad, and his parents were married in St. John's. Chaplin was born in 1889 and died in 1977, just the same as Olave, B.-P.'s wife. He was actually born on 16th April, as was B.-P.'s youngest daughter Betty, her future husband, and their future son! (Chaplin's stolen coffin was later found ten miles from the Swiss cemetery where he had been buried, on Mafeking Day 1978.)

Architect Sir Giles Gilbert Scott's father, George Gilbert Scott, designed the main buildings of Dulwich College (Scoutmaster Marsh's former school). He is buried in Westminster Abbey (although his son Giles designed Liverpool Anglican Cathedral, the largest cathedral in Britain, he was in fact a Catholic). George Scott is remembered in stone in the Abbey along with B.-P., Olave Baden-Powell, Rudyard Kipling, Field-Marshall Plumer (of the Boer War, later Chief Scout for Malta) and General Booth, founder of the SA - not **S**cout **A**ssociation but the **S**alvation **A**rmy. Booth died in the same year and month as the Leysdown tragedy; his daughter Emma was born on the 8th January (B.-P. would die on the **8th January**), his son Ballington was born in **1857**. The Salvation Army, along with numerous other organisations, ran their own Scout Groups.

Parts of the waters around the Leysdown area were more treacherous than people liked to believe. It was recorded in the *East Kent Gazette* (August 1912) that at nearly the same spot twenty years earlier two sons of the Rev. Dickson, rector of Eastchurch, and two sons of the Rev. Farbrother, Vicar of Leysdown, were capsized by a sudden gust of wind. Rev. Dickson's two sons were drowned and one of Rev. Farbrother's also. Alas, in nearby Elmley in 1897, the paper continues, three men and one woman were drowned when their boat overturned. The day following the inquest, the landlord of the inn at Elmley (where the inquest was held), lost his life through his boat capsizing. A few weeks later the foreman of the jury was drowned with another man at Elmley...

From the Birmingham Scout Exhibition of 1913, the
Sea Scouts would prove to be a popular branch of Scouting

A Family of Baby and Cubs

The Walworth Scouts were really early Sea Scouts, the section having followed on from a special camp in 1909 for 100 boys which B.-P. ran at Bucklers Hard, Hampshire. Adjacent to the river Hamble, 50 boys camped on land for one week, then swapped with the 50 boys who had been aboard C. B. Fry's training ship *Mercury*. It was Fry's, the famous cricketer and athlete's, wife who had more control over the running of the TS *Mercury*. She was said to have run a harsh system (at least one cadet died under her regime). The amazing C. B. Fry had done everything from nude modelling, representing England in football, athletics and cricket, and had once taught at Charterhouse.

B.-P.'s son Peter was born in 1913, exactly a year after B.-P.'s wedding. Peter was something of a sickly child, born on the same day as Donald Baden-Powell's mother's funeral (Donald was B.-P.'s nephew). She died early, aged 47, and sadly Peter would also die early at 49 after suffering from leukaemia (on 9th December 1962 - Sir Arthur Pearson had also died on 9th December). Peter had found it difficult living in his father's shadow, but became his own man. He did much to encourage and promote the 'BP Guild', a section for older people who wanted to support the movement but not necessarily directly as warranted leaders.

Peter was too young to become a member of the movement's latest section, called Wolf Cubs. Younger boys had been clamouring to join the Scouts, and some Scoutmasters had opened unofficial 'Junior' Troops to accommodate them. Wolf Cubs were trialled from 1914 but officially launched in 1916 after B.-P. had written a special training programme and handbook for them based on Kipling's *Jungle Book* stories. With their totem poles and wolf's head, they would call out dyb, dyb, dyb and dob, dob, dob - do your best, done our best - and, before it was rude!, give a two-fingered salute (such things came to an end in an historic year for the movement: 1967). Traditionally known as the first registered Wolf Cub Pack was the 1st Westminster, Peter's Own. It was named after B.-P.'s son, who was taken as a baby to view the Pack with his father. In fact the 1st Westminster had been trialling junior Scouting/Cubbing before the scheme was launched, and B.-P. had invited them to tea at his home in Kensington, at 32 Prince's Gate.

Kipling's son, John, had attended the Sea Scout camp on the TS *Mercury*. Sadly, as about a quarter of the Brownsea boys were destined to do, he would lose his life during the Great War. Kipling, though, remained a good supporter of the Wolf Cubs and generously allowed B.-P. to use his work as he saw fit.

One wonders, highly popular as the Cub section proved to be, if it did not have an impact on the success and numbers of the Scout section. From the 1940s, in fact, there have always been more Cubs than Scouts in the movement (on the other hand, since 1921 there have always been more Girl Guides than Boy Scouts in the UK movements).

SIR ROBERT BADEN POWELL 2nd. FROM LEFT, WALKING ROUND THE GROUNDS AT
ALEXANDRA PARK TO INSPECT ARRANGEMENTS FOR SCOUT RALLY..............

Lord Hampton.   Chief Scout.   C.C. Branch.

The Rally was for Wolf Cubs
to welcome the Prince of Wales, 1922.

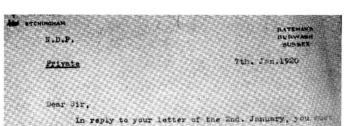

Correspondence from
Rudyard Kipling

N.D.P.

BATEMAN'S
BURWASH
SUSSEX

Private

7th. Jan.1920

Dear Sir,

In reply to your letter of the 2nd. January, you must
remember that among wolves, the Head-wolf's name is always
one that can be howled easily, so as to be heard at a long
AKELA
distance. "A-kela", therefore, is A-KAY- LAH, with the
accent on the second syllable which can be prolonged indef-
initely . The initial A, on the other hand, is almost a grunt
- "Er". Try this as a howl and you will see the beauty of it

Faithfully yours,

Rudyard Kipling

The 1st. Forest Hill to greet The Prince.

October 7th., is to be a great day for
Scouts and Cubs for H.R.H. The Prince of
Wales is going to inspect 50,000 Scouts and
10,000 Cubs at Alexandra Palace. And of
course the "Foresters" must be there in full
strength.

We shall travel by Charabanc leaving
Forest Hill (Westbourne Road) at 12.30
pick up our City friends at Coleman Street,
(Gresham Street end) at 1.15, arriving at
the Palace about 2 o'clock. As a number of
parents and friends have expressed a desire
to see the rally, I will make arrangements
to hire another charabanc, only I must know
in good time, the number going. The cost
will be 2/6 Return for Scouts and Cubs, and
3/6 for Adults. (Children under 14 years
same price as scouts.)

Tickets are now on sale, and as the
seating accommodation is limited, you should
secure your ticket now.

Above: At Alexandra Palace ~
a nervous Peter with his mum and dad

The First World War and Beyond

The Scouts proved themselves to be the salt of the earth during the 1st World War. They were able to help with all manner of things, including: coastguard duties, sounding the All-Clear, delivering messages, collecting salvage, and guarding railway lines and reservoirs. Woe betide anyone who didn't take them seriously. For example, one man thought he would test the mettle of a Scout by climbing a telegraph pole and refusing to answer questions. He found his bicycle tyres slashed (to hamper his getaway) and the news that a policeman would be arriving shortly.

In 1917 the Prime Minister, Lloyd George, himself gave praise to the Boy Scout movement:

I do not think I am exaggerating when I say that the young boyhood of our country, represented by the Boy Scouts Association, shares the laurels for having been prepared with the old and trusted British Army and Navy. For both proved their title to make a claim when the Great War broke upon us like a thief in the night. It is no small matter to be proud of that the Association was able within a month of the outbreak of war to give the most energetic and intelligent help in all kinds of service. When the boyhood of a nation can give such practical proofs of its honour, straightness and loyalty, there is not much danger of that nation going under, for these boys are in training to render service to their country as leaders in all walks of life in the future.

B.-P. had done his bit too. When not keeping up morale in England, both he and Olave had gone out to the Front and worked in the soldiers' recreation huts the Scouts and Guides had bought through their fundraising efforts (they also donated Scout and Guide ambulances to carry wounded soldiers). The gossip was that B.-P.'s time in Etaples and elsewhere was all a cover for his spying activities!

The movement would provide Britain with her youngest-ever holder of the Victoria Cross. Founded by Queen Victoria, the first one was presented in the year of B.-P.'s birth, **1857**. In 1916 it would be posthumously awarded to a former Boy Scout of east London, John Travers Cornwell. The *Black Prince* and other battle cruisers were sunk in the Battle of Jutland. 'Jack' Cornwell, serving on HMS *Chester,* with those all around him dying and despite receiving horrific injuries himself, remained positioned at his gun. His injuries were attended to back in Grimsby hospital by Dr. Stephenson (coincidentally one of B.-P.'s middle names) but he died shortly afterwards. His body was brought back to London and buried in an unmarked common grave. A press campaign and wide support from his native East Ham and West Ham resulted in his body being exhumed and honourably reburied in almost royal fashion in Manor Park cemetery. With a special Scout badge named in his honour by B.-P., and with local fame, he grew into a folk hero. (It has taken nearly a century for the full facts to be known: numerous eminent sources and institutions over the years have stated incorrectly that Cornwell was buried in Grimsby; nor do they mention his first burial in an unmarked grave in London.)

Left: The courageous Cornwell,
from a painting by Frank Salisbury

SIXES AND EIGHTS....

Jack Cornwell was born on the **8th January** 1900, a time when B.-P. was occupied with his Mafeking undertakings. B.-P. would not see out the duration of the Second World War, dying on the **8th January** 1941.

B.-P.'s Commander-in-Chief, Lord Roberts, earned his VC during the siege of Lucknow, in the year of B.-P.'s birth. Lord Roberts' son, a Lieutenant in the King's Royal Rifles, was posthumously awarded the VC for his bravery in the Battle of Colenso, South Africa, 1899. He was born on the **8th January** 1872.

As part of the 600 recruits, Jack Cornwell trained for his naval service at Keyham Naval Barracks, Plymouth. He was quartered in Mess 6. He was aged sixteen and six months when he died in the sixth month of 1916. Awarded the Victoria Cross, this had been instituted with a royal warrant in 1856 (the following year Queen Victoria, in Hyde Park, personally presented 62 winners of the VC on 26th June).

There were an estimated 6000 killed in the Battle of Jutland. There were six boys in total who, during the battle, lost their lives aboard the HMS *Chester*. Whilst serving his country, Jack's father died soon after his son, aged 63. Many roads, buildings and institutions were named after the keen former Boy Scout of Manor Park who became a hero of Jutland. In the year following his death, a bronze memorial plaque was erected at Walton Road school, one of Jack's former schools, it being unveiled by Lady Jellicoe, wife of Earl Jellicoe, on 16th July.

In 2006 a Jack Cornwell commemorative stamp was released by the Post Office as part of a set of 6 stamps. By that year there had been a total of 1,356 VCs awarded.

Despite the war, in 1917 Betty, the youngest of the B.-P. family was born (Peter, Heather and Betty all now living at 'Pax Hill', in **B**entley **P**arish, Hampshire). It was also the year the movement was able to move from Victoria Street to newly built premises - larger and what became their permanent premises - in Buckingham Palace Road. **BP** Road! though sadly it would be the day news of the death of Scout artist Ernest Carlos was received (see next page). The Girl Guides would later occupy premises a few doors down at number 17 (and are still there today). The Scouts, at number 25, shared the building with the Madras and Southern Mahratta Railway Company (it may have brought back memories for B.-P.!). It was from here that the Equipment Department, which became the Association's main Scout Shop branch, operated. Strangely, when the Scout Association moved from BP Road to co-locate at Baden-Powell House, leaving just the Scout Shop, they were asked by the Post Office to alter their number to 27 BP Road.

With the war finally ending at the eleventh hour, on the eleventh day of the eleventh month of 1918, the Scout movement, which had seen a rise in popularity and membership among boys during the war, could turn to addressing issues and tasks that had been put on hold or delayed at the onset of war.

A Jamboree to mark the movement's tenth anniversary (1908 - 1918) had had to be postponed but could now be planned for. This, the world's first Scout Jamboree, was held at London's Olympia, and had Scouts from Britain and all over the world attending (some Scouts' fathers had even fought on the side of the Boers in the South African War). It was a spectacular show open to the public for eight days, and had a small zoo, massed Scout choir, demonstrations of rescue, flying, national dances, physical training and much more. B.-P.'s reasons for holding the Jamboree were, among other things, to remember those who had lost their lives in the war, to mark the restoration of peace and to ~

invite our brother Scouts from overseas, not only those who are our close allies but those who remained neutral and even those who were for the time being our enemies, where they exist.

Although B.-P. was obviously a member of the movement he'd created, he was not a Scoutmaster, did not hold a Scouter's warrant and did not really have a grand enough title for what had so quickly become a world-wide movement. How appropriate, then, that on the last day of the Jamboree, August 7th, he should be declared Chief Scout of the World. The Jamboree had been a huge success in PR terms though nearly bankrupted the movement, despite thousands visiting it daily.

The 1920s were something of a golden era for Scouting. Despite the bond of grief after the Great War, the shortage of materials (Scouts would be asked to bring their own sugar to camp in the early twenties), Scouting offered local, affordable recreation that was fun and purposeful (it also provided a significant degree of social care and moral education too). The movement catered for a wide age-range (a wider age-range than all other youth organisations catered for until some of them too expanded) several nights a week and at weekends as well. The introduction of the Rover Scout section in 1917 meant the movement also catered for young men of 17 to 24 (the lower and upper age limits altered over time). The Rover Scouts (former Prime Minister Sir Harold Wilson had been a keen King's/Rover Scout, his father was a Rover Scout leader) were seen as a way of keeping young men in the movement and improving the chances of supplying the various sections with leaders (often in short supply). Similarly, the movement, popular in preparatory schools, was finally able to seep into the public schools: Eton being one of, if not the, first to set the trend and help train up the Scoutmasters and Commissioners of tomorrow.

Born in 1883, Ernest Stafford Carlos trained at Lambeth Art School and the Royal Academy School of Art. He saw great potential in the new boys' movement - the Scouts - and became a keen Scoutmaster. In his short career his Scout paintings became very popular, especially one of 1913, titled *The Pathfinder* (left). It can be seen (as a copy) on the wall of fictional Ken Barlow's home in *Coronation Street*. A stained glass window of the picture can be seen in Holy Cross Church, Hornchurch, Essex, where Carlos's elder brother was the first vicar. Ernest Carlos would sadly die fighting for his country during the First World War.

BOY SCOUTS'
International Jamboree

THE DAILY GRAPHIC.

SCOUTS ARE OF ALL SIZES, SHAPES

JULY 31st
to
AUG. 7th
1920

OLYMPIA
11 a.m. to 9 p.m.

ARENA PERFORMANCES
2.30 and 7 p.m.

Official
Programme
1/- NET.

PRINTED AND PUBLISHED BY
GALE & POLDEN LTD., 2 AMEN CORNER, E.C. 4
ALDERSHOT & PORTSMOUTH

Copyright

Left: Programme, cover
designed by John Hassall

Inside Olympia

Gilwell Park and the Halcyon Days of the 1920s

In 1919 the movement acquired its first official national campsite and leader training centre - Gilwell Park. It was a rundown estate situated on the edge of Epping Forest, Essex - a place Sir Arthur Pearson knew well through his already established Fresh Air Fund for deprived children, who visited Epping Forest on their numerous excursions. Even in its first year his Fresh Air Fund took 20,000 East End kids for picnics in Epping Forest (it still exists today as Pearson's Holiday Fund). A wealthy Scottish businessman - and Scout Commissioner - William de Bois Maclaren (another publisher who was to help B.-P.), had offered to give £7000 to purchase a suitable camping ground and training school (intended primarily for London's East End Scouts). The almost derelict Georgian country house (built in 1771, it later became known as the White House) with 57 or so acres of grounds was eventually discovered for sale at precisely £7000. It was promptly purchased, and Maclaren added a further £3000 to renovate the main Hall/White House residence.

It was at Gilwell that the Wood Badge training scheme for leaders was developed. Gilwell itself was officially opened in the **seventh** month of 1919 with a rally of **700** Scouts in attendance, along with B.-P., Maclaren and his wife, who cut the ribbons in the Scout colours of green and yellow. Only three years later the Guides accepted the generous offer of Foxlease Park, another country house next to another forest - the New Forest - which they used (and still use) as their main campsite and training centre. It was later discovered that the property had once belonged to a member of the Baden-Powell family.

The White House is a grade II listed building (over the years it has been reputed to be haunted). When in the ownership of the wealthy Chinnery family, they entertained lavishly - King George VI was a regular visitor. George Chinnery, the owner's brother, was a well known painter. He left his wife, declaring her *'the ugliest woman I have ever seen'*. Trying to keep his wife at a distance, he travelled aboard a trading ship bound for Madras. It was called the *Gilwell*.

But the Scouts' Gilwell, although quite primitive in the early twenties, became a special place for B.-P. (he later kept his 'Eccles'caravan there) and Scouts. Local Scouts on foot, cycle or with trek-cart would flock there most weekends; Scouts from further afield and, very soon, Scouts and leaders from all over the world also camped at this unique place. The late Bill Copping, before becoming general manager of the Scout Shop in Victoria, admitted that as a junior sales assistant he would often race away from the Scout Shop on a Friday evening and head for Gilwell. All he bought with him was a tin mug.

I used to sidle over to any group with a fire going. A comment such as "I see the kettle's on" would soon get a welcome cup of tea. I don't know how, I never brought a tent and yet

I always managed to find a place to kip somewhere. I loved the place.

It was quite common, when attending a leaders' Wood Badge course, to have in your Patrol Scouters from India, Australia and many other countries (trainees were required to camp and live as a typical Boy Scout unit - a Patrol consisting of six to eight members.

(The King v. Chinnery.)

GILLWELL HOUSE and Estate, in ESSEX;
AND
Freehold Warehouse, in Vine-street, near the Strand.

TO BE SOLD,
TO THE BEST BIDDER,

Pursuant to Two several Orders of His Majesty's Court of Exchequer, made on the 3ᵈ day of July 1812, in a Matter between Our Sovereign Lord *The King* and *William Chinnery*, on several Writs of Extent, before ABEL MOYSEY, Esquire, the Deputy to His Majesty's Remembrancer of the said Court,

AT THE EXCHEQUER OFFICE, IN THE INNER TEMPLE,
LONDON,

On Thursday, the 8ᵗʰ day of April next,
AT TWELVE O'CLOCK AT NOON,

IN FOUR LOTS,

AN ELEGANT VILLA,
And an Eligible and very Improveable

Freehold Estate,
Situate in the Hamlet of
SEWARDSTONE, in the Parish of WALTHAM-HOLY-CROSS,
in the County of ESSEX,
Surrounded by the beautiful Scenery of
EPPING FOREST,
And only Twelve Miles from London, through Walthamstow and Chinkford, and about Three Miles from Waltham Abbey.

Gilwell was originally spelt Gillwell, but the spelling of today was settled when B.-P. took the name when made a peer in 1929: Lord Baden-Powell of Gilwell.

According to a Bill of Auction in 1906, Gilwell was due to have a handy railway station: *Note: An Act has passed the Second Reading for the construction of the N.E. London Railway and when this railway is completed a station to be known as Gilwell Park Station will be within a few minutes of the property.* (Chingford would be the name of the nearest station, and it was hardly just round the corner!)

The White House

Earliest records for Gilwell go back to 1407, with a listed dwelling on the site known as Gyldiefords. Alas, too early to benefit from Scout training, around 1736 highwayman Dick Turpin would know Gilwell and the surrounding area well, eventually becoming very familiar with the Hangman's knot!

Pioneer Boy Scout campers
before Gilwell days.

By the 1920s thousands upon thousands of boys had enjoyed camping out locally, further afield and even abroad - few would have had such opportunities for travel and camaraderie before joining the Scouts.

B.-P. was the Chief Scout of the World, and he created a Camp Chief to oversee the training of Scoutmasters. Pearson was known as the 'Chief' in his publishing empire, and it would be another chief who supplied B.-P. with his idea for awarding successful candidates a leather thong with two wooden beads attached. The original 'Wood Badge' beads presented to successful course participants, had come from the necklace of captured Zulu chief Dinizulu (he was sentenced to ten years' banishment on St. Helena - former exile home of Napoleon - for high treason).

The magical spirit of Gilwell, away from the committee and accounts men of BP Road, was imbibed by thousands upon thousands of members over many decades. Camping, camp-fires, cooking over golden embers, singsongs, swimming, carving, rope-spinning, trekking, comradeship, reunions - it all happened at Gilwell. What B.-P. would make of Gilwell Park today, with its CCTV, boxes of risk assessment forms, along with the new Scout Association office block deposited there (no doubt a necessary decision) I'm not so sure. Always in fear of his movement becoming paper-bound and an 'organisation', he wrote about this, not for the first time, in his regular *Outlook* column in 1936:

Personally, I fear there is a danger that a kind of synthetic Scouting may creep into our training in place of the natural article described in Scouting for Boys ... By 'synthetic Scouting' I mean the Scout system obscured by overclothing the natural form with rules and instructive literature, tending to make what originally was, and should be, an open air game into a science for the Scouter and a school curriculum for the boy.

I think of this so often when people write to me asking for something to be written into the rules so that they can do it. Get on with it, is my reply, then let me know if it is a good idea so that I can pass it on. If everything we can do was put into the rule book it would fill a library.

Early Scout
transport

Many of those who were involved in the siege of Mafeking, remembered it year by year, as did the Chief...

"*If anybody says he is not afraid of those shells he is — a burly liar!*"

(Overheard)
10.11.99

MAFEKING DAY, 1928.

PAX HILL.

Lunch at 1.30 p.m.

DEFENCE

Lord Charles Bentinck
Colonel G. Bridges
Lady Godley
Sir Alexander Godley
Colonel Greener
Major Holmden
Brig.-Gen. C. Ryan
Sir Hubert Swinburne
Mr. B. Weil
Mr. F. Whiteley
Sir Tom Bridges
Lady Sarah Wilson
Sir R. Baden-Powell

ABSENT

Sir Courtenay Vyvyan
Col. T. Greenfield

MENU.

Consommé Royale.

Mayonnaise de Saumon.

Poulet de Surrey Rôti.
Soufflé de Volaille au Truffée.
Jambon de York.
Salade Russe.
Salade des Pommes de Terre.

Compôte de Fruits à la Chantilly.
Bombe Glacé Praline.

Country Dancing
by the Bentley Team.

TRAINS TO LONDON.		
Leave Bentley.		Arrive London.
4-38	....	6-19
5-32	....	6-49
5-58	....	7-51

RELIEF

Major B. Baden-Powell
Lady Charles Bentinck
Sir Alfred Edwards
Sir Edward Garraway
Col. Geoffrey Glyn
Col. Weston Jarvis
Col. Courage
Col. Hoel Llewellyn
Sir Alfred Fripp
Major Tomlinson
Col. H. P. Sykes
Lady Baden-Powell

ABSENT

F.M. Lord Plumer
Sir Bryan Mahon
Major S. Weil
General P. Rolt

Other highs of the twenties include the Scout Migration scheme, explorer Sir Ernest Shackleton's extraordinary invitation for two boys to join him on his Antarctic expedition, and the 1929 'Coming of Age' Jamboree. The first of these subjects, emigration, saw Scouts leaving for Canada and Australia almost on a monthly basis at times, to live and work with a farming family while they were trained in various aspects of farm work.

In 1921, out of a selection process involving 1,700 Boy Scouts, two places were offered for Shackleton's expedition. He had originally only offered one place but after interviewing the final ten applicants he sent a telegram saying *'Shackleton selecting Marr and Mooney, but wanted to take the lot'*. Ultimately it was the 17 year-old Marr who lasted the whole voyage. Coincidentally both boys were from Scotland and neither was a Sea Scout. It certainly proved to be a rough time, with most of the experienced crew succumbing to sea-sickness. As he later recalled, even Marr couldn't avoid some flowery language during one particularly trying period, as joint biographers of Shackleton, M and J. Fisher, reveal:

'I was a filthy mess of porridge from all these pots and pans and I lost my temper. The cook had packed up and I felt to hell with this. Although I was a Boy Scout I was no prude. I burst into a stream of the most filthiest obscenity and abuse and profanity, as I was trying to collect all the pots and pans and put them back in the galley to wash and they were all scurrying up and down in the waist of the ship. I was really giving a very good exhibition, one a sailor would have been proud of if he'd been listening - and indeed somebody was, for Shackleton poked his head out of his cabin to see what the noise was and saw the Boy Scout. I remember I just glanced round, and he smiled and went back in his cabin.'

A day or two later Marr was cleaning out Shackleton's cabin when he came in and offered the boy an extra pound a week, to help him, as he said, with his fees in the Granite City. He told Marr he was shaping up well, and Marr felt sure that the exhibition of his fluency had helped to form Shackleton's opinion of him.

Sadly, the 'Boss' Shackleton himself would not last the whole voyage, as he died of a coronary thrombosis aboard his ship at the age of 47. (He was a former Dulwich College

pupil, and his brother had been a contemporary there with C. B. Fry's brother.) Shackleton's wife was a leader in the Girl Guide movement, at one time a Guide Commissioner in Eastbourne from 1917 to 1927.

Left: Shackleton nearest the camera, with Scouts Marr and (far right) Mooney, having set sail on **17**th September.

Shackleton's famous compatriot, Captain Robert Falcon Scott, had not survived his heroic South Pole expedition of 1912, his position as President of the Camping Club was left vacant for some years but was eventually filled by B.-P. Members of the club were often seen camping on the large lawn at Pax Hill, the B.-P.s' home in the village of Bentley, Hampshire; the founder's grandson, Robert, became President in 1992. The son of Robert Scott, the famous ornithologist and artist Sir Peter Scott, became a keen Scout at West Downs school (he was born and lived in 174 Buckingham Palace Road, not far from the Boy Scout Association's head offices!). For the movement, the 7th October 1937 was a glorious day when it proudly accepted his father's former expeditionary ship RSS *Discovery*. It was moored on the Thames and used as a training base for Sea Scouts.

The late twenties would see a life peerage for B.-P., he choosing the title Lord Baden-Powell of Gilwell; and the 1929 Jamboree held in Arrowe Park, Birkenhead, surpassed all others. With 71 separate contingents, and attended by 30,000 Scouts, the kudos of the movement (there were now 4 million Scouts and Guides world-wide) can be seen by the fact that both the Prince of Wales - the future King - and the Prime Minister visited the Jamboree, and the Archbishop of Canterbury came to bless the proceedings.

Like Jamboree participants of today, for many of the lucky Boy Scouts of 1929 the opportunity to attend the Jamboree was the chance of a lifetime. A sprightly ninety-four year old South Londoner recently recalled: *Times were hard then, we were grateful to the Woolich Rotary Club, who helped us out by buying new scarves for all the boys attending the Jamboree. We went up by special train, and met people from all over the world. It is a trip that has stayed with me ever since.*

During part of the Jamboree the 'B.-P. weather' quickly churned the ground into a bog of lumpy gravy, but B.-P. was always positive and optimistic. He remarked on one of the days: *'You see, any ass can be a Scout on a fine day, but the thing is to make the best of conditions on a bad day'.*

Through Scouts from all over the world collecting pennies to buy a gift for their founder, B.-P. was presented with a Rolls Royce, a portrait of himself by David Jagger RA (painter of Queen Mary and other eminent people) and a pair of braces - when Olave had discreetly asked what present he would like, he'd only wanted a pair of braces. The Rolls Royce (in private ownership today) was nicknamed Jam Roll, playing on the words Jamboree and Rolls Royce; it came complete with a second gift of an 'Eccles' caravan.

His press secretary of the time recalled how B.-P. was standing in the Royal Box watching a rehearsal when he became irritated with a pesky photographer.

Hundreds of spectators became convulsed with laughter:

After a while Baden-Powell told him to go. The man continued pestering and to the delight of those who saw it, Baden-Powell, then over 70, chased the man out of the arena.

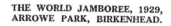

THE WORLD JAMBOREE, 1929,
ARROWE PARK, BIRKENHEAD.

The bearer *General Sir Elliott Wood*

has permission to pass into Camp, for the purpose of

admittance to the Royal Box on 10th. August.

G. Walton

World Jamboree, 1929.

Below: One of the thousands of overseas campers

An earlier car of B.-P.'s, a Standard (note the number plate!).
Taken during a visit to a Camping Club site, 1922.

Crest of a Wave Through Hard Times

The initials RAF were, on more than one occasion, jovially said to stand for Reader's Air Force, for he became well known during the Second World War for staging morale-boosting Gang Shows. These RAF Gang Shows helped to kick-start the professional showbiz careers of numerous actors, including Peter Sellers, Richard Attenborough and Tony Hancock. Ralph Reader's fame had spread a decade or so before this, however, as a Broadway and West End producer and also the producer of a new form of Scout entertainment and fundraiser: the Scout Gang Show. It certainly beat singsongs in the park or jumble sales, and despite the harsh times of the Depression, Gang Shows proved to be a new and vibrant wing in Scout fundraising activities.

No longer a household name today, Ralph Reader was in many ways (for a time at least) the Andrew Lloyd Weber of the 1930s. Yet he came from humble roots - born to Salvation Army folk in Somerset, orphaned at nine, and with suspected TB. He'd caught the showbiz bug very young, by seeing occasional shows at the Brighton Hippodrome. He could never have predicted that his own Gang Shows would be sell-outs, put on at the Golders Green Hippodrome in front of the Queen and a host of other famous people.

It all started with an invitation by a relative who invited the rather green teenager to come out to America and try his luck in show business there. He stayed at **217** (back to Mafeking!), 76th Street, 3rd Avenue, and did office work whilst trying for auditions, which were mostly unsuccessful to begin with. But within a short space of time Ralph Reader had nine shows playing on Broadway.

His first London Gang Show was put on at the Scala Theatre in 1932, and had B.-P. attending the opening night. From a shaky start where the tickets were practically given away, the London Gang Show became an annual institution and had many regional spin-offs. Reader's own creation was heard and seen by thousands through the sale of LPs, and excerpts on radio, Royal Command performances and television. In 1937 the Gang Show was even made into a film at Pinewood Studios. A story at the time concerned Marlene Dietrich, who was watching the filming of *The Gang Show*. During a break she offered to take four boys to lunch in the studio restaurant. Someone enquired if she had a preference for the ages of the boys, to which she is alleged to have commented: *"Vell, for lunch, about thirteen or fourteen, but for supper, twenty-one!"*

"We're riding along on the crest of a wave."

Above: Ralph Reader at the 1951 El Alamein Reunion, with Sir Winston Churchill,
Field Marshall Montgomery and General Eisenhower.

Above: Towards the end of his career, with some of the Gang Show cast

The Veteran Soldier Winds Down

1937 can really be viewed as the end of B.-P. taking an active role in the movement: the Boy Scouts were phased-in from 1907 and his active association with it phased-out after his attendance at the 1937 Jamboree held in Holland (it would be his last Jamboree). Although eighty years of age (with symptoms of skin cancer and other health complaints) he was still able to mount his charger and proudly inspect the 27,000 Boy Scout campers who had gathered from around the world. After the horrific scenes of the First World War, B.-P. had always seen the Jamboree (usually held every four years) as the chance to encourage peace - for the youth of nations to come together and put aside barriers of class, religion and race. Tim Jeal, to me, conjures up a picture of a 'white Gandhi' when he comments on B.-P. and the Jamborees of his later years:

Most of his major speeches were filmed and the sight of an old man in shorts with a benign expression urging tolerance and fraternal goodwill upon his vast international audiences still has the power to move. The way in which these huge crowds of boys warmed to him, cheering his words and waving hats and staves aloft, is very poignant when one remembers that such scenes took place on the eve of a war in which so many of them would die. In 1938 Baden-Powell's name was submitted to the Nobel Peace Prize Committee for consideration for the following year's award. But the 1939 Prize would turn out to be one of Hitler's many unnoticed casualties.

The commissioner overleaf (1913) has obviously worked hard or been financially generous, as three 'Thanks' badges can be seen. Much can be made of B.-P. handing out these Swastika badges for good help and support but the design had been used years before it was taken up by Hitler (which is when B.-P. ceased to use it). In 1908, for example, the London jewellers Elkingtons sold a range of Swastika pendants set in diamonds (they were a symbol of good luck, prosperity and long life). The symbol can also be seen in early published books by Rudyard Kipling.

Other organisations also adopted the ancient symbol (in Sanskrit meaning good fortune or well being). In 1910, however, it was used as an incentive for people to help fund the movement. Launching the Boy Scouts' Appeal Fund, the *Daily Telegraph* announced that bronze, silver and gold Swastika Thanks badges (which they also called 'Badges of Honour') would be presented to every giver of an annual subscription for three years. The 'pecking order' was: gold for £5.00, silver for £1.00 , and bronze for 10s.

Although the Dutch Jamboree was B.-P.'s last major Scout event, he did attend the last special Scout and Guide Cruise with Olave and 700 happy cruisers aboard the *Orduna* in 1938. The first of three such cruises had been aboard the *Calgaric* in 1933. They had been the idea of Olave. **BP** had been the place - Bucze in Poland - when Olave, attending the **seventh** World Guide Conference, commented to a friend how she would like to take a ship-load of Guiders to see what was going on in other countries. (In private correspondence around this time Olave remarked on a perceived difference in how she and B.-P. were received on visits in the UK and abroad. When overseas they were still treated like royalty, but less so on home soil.) A visit by B.-P. to the offices of the White Star Line (on other business) ended with B.-P. asking casually, "Why can't you find us a ship for our Guide and Scout cruise?"

And so it was, with Scout and Guide flags flying proudly, the *Calgaric* left Southampton for a cruise of the Baltic. Replete with 475 Guiders, 100 Scouters, and 80 friends and relations, the cruisers visited 9 countries in 17 days. The low number of Scouters on this first cruise was mainly due to many having already committed leave and money to attend the Scout Jamboree in Hungary. It was undoubtedly highly pleasurable to be travelling in the company of the Chief Scout and World Chief Guide, but the whole cruise was a 'Scouty' affair, as can be gleaned from Eileen Wade's biography of Olave:

This was to be cruising with an object. It would be something far more than the mere sight-seeing, feasting, and propping up of the bar of the ordinary cruise, though all of these pleasures would be available. But there would be few idle moments for anyone. The cruisers were divided into patrols under various leaders who demanded a great deal of them in the way of ingenuity, skill, artistic effort, dramatics, singing and dancing, games and lectures - all entertainment in fact to be provided by the cruisers themselves - and in the event this turned out to be of a very high calibre.

When reading about the cruises (and there were also Scout train cruises in the UK too) and seeing early photographs of men and boys in baggy shorts singing around a campfire, it is difficult to see the Scouts as a paramilitary organisation. The early criticism of militarism directed at the Scouts, which has continued from time to time throughout most of its history, was largely without foundation (although a small minority of Scoutmasters attempted to train their Scouts along military lines in the earliest years).

It was always going to be a difficult label to shift, B.-P. had become a military brand name: inextricably linked with war and the army through the media well before the foundation of the Scouts. He was a military hero, the saviour of Mafeking, a conquering soldier, a famous colonel. Before and after 1907 he could be eyeballed in full military dress at Madame Tussauds (eventually the uniform was exchanged for a Scout one, and he is still exhibited there today). If B.-P. had wanted youths to undertake a more military style of training, he would have had a much stronger allegiance with organisations such as the Cadets and Church Lads' Brigade. Other organisations, such as the YMCA and Salvation Army, would not have embraced B.-P.'s scheme if they had had any fears over militarism.

Militarism was really only in the eye of the beholder. The veteran MP and peace campaigner Tony Benn first visited the House of Commons in 1937 (it happened to be the **22nd of February**). Yet as a boy he was a keen member of the 52nd Westminster Scout Troop, later writing in his autobiography:

I loved the Boy Scouts and my Scoutmaster, Godfrey Barber, was a pacifist, a good, kind man. We had a Scout camp in Oban, Scotland, and lived in tents. Mr Barber developed a 'wet latrine' where, instead of peeing into the ground, he got us to cut a little trench and fill it with pebbles. We stood by the trench and peed into it, protected from public view by a canvas screen just in front of the trench.

When a Scout Commissioner came to see us he made use of this, but totally misunderstood the principle, and stood on the pebbles and peed against the canvas screen. He declared he had never seen such a good Scout latrine!

When I decided that, with the approach of war, I should transfer from the Scouts to the Air Training Corps, Mr Barber was very disappointed....

The Second World War and Passing of B.-P.

As in the 1st World War, many Scouts (Guides also) before being called up served the war effort by helping at harvest camps, with evacuation, as hospital orderlies, erecting shelters, collecting salvage and running messages. For young lads the work ranged from being tedious and tiring - simply being available and on call - to witnessing horrific scenes when helping to rescue people from bombed buildings and at casualty stations. Occasional mild exploitation, later seen after the Bob-a-Job scheme was introduced in 1949, occurred. The following example concerned Scouts based at Romford Town Hall. Scout Alfred Reeve was working with fellow Scouts to get his War Service badge. Working in shifts, regardless of air-raids they were on call night and day, ready to deliver urgent messages. He recalls:

There was the occasional air-raid and we became adept at judging the exact moment to swerve into shelter, whether by lying flat beside a garden wall or crouched against the side of a house as bombers released their loads above. Over our dark blue battle blouses we wore a webbing harness with a pouch in the front. This held the front lamp of our bike and was a clever arrangement which left our hands free at all times and meant we didn't have to detach the lamp from the bike when we got off.

Early one morning we heard explosions in the distance. There were four Scouts on duty, asleep on our bunks in the stand-by quarters. The first sirens sounded and we wondered if we were going to be called. The phone shrilled and when the senior messenger answered it we were told to report at once. On arrival, Jack [the man in charge] *handed us each a batch of envelopes, already sorted for routes and destinations.*

He pulled aside the blackout curtain which hung in front of the door and looked up at the sky. "This could be a nasty one but I'm told these messages are urgent. Don't take chances but do the best you can."

It was a 'nasty one' but we delivered our messages without casualties although with a great deal of trepidation as we sped along streets lit only by the flashes of anti-aircraft gun-fire.

It struck me at the time that we delivered to some curious addresses - curious in the fact that they were quite ordinary houses. It was not until the following week that I learned of the storm that had blown up over our errand. Our 'urgent' messages had been, unbeknown to Jack, invitations to the Mayor's tea party which his secretary had forgotten to post. She had had the bright idea of using the Civil Defence messengers, unfortunately on what turned out to be one of the worst air raids of the year.

Former Boy Scout and commissioner, Guy Gibson, would lead the successful Dam Busters raid and be posthumously awarded the VC. The *Minotaur,* a boat belonging to the 1st Mortlake Sea Scouts, was skippered by one of their leaders and used as part of the 'little ships rescue' at Dunkirk (as was a lifeboat purchased for the RNLI by the Girl Guides and later named *Guide of Dunkirk*). During Guide Gift Week held in 1940, in fact, Girl Guides of Britain and the Empire raised £59, 296. 3. 4d for the war effort.

B.-P., in his eighties and very unwell, would leave with Olave in 1938 to stay in the warmer climes of his beloved Nyeri, never to return. 'Paxtu', their retirement bungalow had been built for them by Eric Walker, a close friend and former Scout Inspector of 1908. B.-P.'s daughter Heather would finally get her father's approval to marry - she married John King, a one time goalkeeper for Charterhouse.

The B.-P.s' home was next to the Outspan Hotel and close to its lodge known as Treetops (this being the place where Princess Elizabeth had been staying when she heard the news of her father's death and learnt that she would be Queen). For B.-P., against the backdrop of snowcapped Mount Kenya, some 17,000 feet high, he described his time in Nyeri to Eileen Wade, his secretary of 27 years, thus: *'as near to perfection as one can get in this world '.*

B.-P.'s Christmas card of 1940 would be his last. It read:

Out of evil good will come. We owe a statue to Hitler, he has done more than any man ever to consolidate our nation at home and overseas and has given us friends in America and in all the countries he has ravaged; such wide friendship will help to bring world peace so soon as he and his war clouds are swept away ... Stick it out! Play up to the Scout's slogan Sleeves up! and with Tails up go to it to win the war, and after that to bring about peace with goodwill and happiness for all.

The 7th of January was really B.-P.'s last full day, in the early hours of the 8th he was barely conscious and died at around 5.00 am. On the 8th January 1908 B.-P. had given a lecture on his Scouting for Boys scheme at the Paddington Baths, just round the corner from where he was born. His new movement was stirring into life. On the 8th January 1941, sadly, his life finally flickered to a close. Eric Walker, his loyal friend, was serving in the war and had been unaware just how close to death the founder was. Upon eventually hearing of B.-P.'s precarious position he obtained leave and, as he records in his book *Treetops Hotel,* hurried back from Eritrea too late:

....arriving only to find him in his coffin in the cottage I had built for him ... I paid him the last service that anyone could. I went to the pantry, collected a duster, and tin of metal polish, and shone up the tarnished plate on the coffin, and am not ashamed to say that with the polish were mixed salt tears.

Left: An example of B.-P.'s artwork.

Below: Part of B.-P.'s funeral cortege.

Memorial services for B.-P. were held throughout the country, and a national memorial service was held in Westminster Abbey on the 27th January. B.-P. was buried in his beloved Nyeri though Olave did not attend the actual funeral (no doubt connected with her double tragedy of losing through suicide, at different times, her father and her sister Auriol).

She called his passing and absence her black despair and was at a loss what to do. She did take over as Chief Guide of Kenya from her friend Lady Brooke-Popham (her initials and those of her husband's mirrored the B.-P.s'. The Governor and Chief Scout of Kenya was Sir **R**obert **B**rooke-**P**opham, his wife was Lady **O**pal **B**rooke-**P**opham).

Olave's England home, Pax Hill, had been requisitioned by the War Department, though she later returned to England and continued to promote both movements from her grace and favour apartment at Hampton Court Palace. Although Bentley had lost its famous General, in 1947 another famous General came to settle in the parish, at nearby Isington Mill. He was Viscount Montgomery of Alamein.

A national appeal fund to build a memorial Scouts' house in central London was started on St. George's Day in 1942. Although the movement raised £**57**,000 for the war effort,

raising sufficient funds for an appropriate memorial home during the difficult conditions of war (and also the very lean times immediately afterwards) proved a mammoth task. A second appeal was launched on the centenary of his birth in 1957, and brought in more funds (though even in 1960 *The Scouter* lamented the fact that out of the 12,000 Scout Groups in the UK, not many more than 2000 had contributed the 3/- that made them automatic 'Founder Groups' of Baden-Powell House). The Camping Club of Great Britain, of which B.-P. had been President, enjoyed a prompter response from its members, which soon resulted in the acquisition of a new memorial campsite in Hertford, which opened in 1953. Called the Baden-Powell site, coincidentally it had previously been the **B**alls **P**ark site.

The Many Georges

B.-P. had a brother called George, he became an MP, and earned a knighthood though sadly died relatively young.

B.-P.'s God-father, from whom he gets two of his names, was the son of a George: the famous engineer George Stephenson.

B.-P. and his mother resided at St. George's Place, SW7.

It was King George V who was the first King to review a national Scout rally (held in Windsor Great Park in 1911).

Gilwell Park overlooks the King George Reservoir.

In 1927 B.-P. was made Knight Grand Cross of Order St. Michael and St. George.

It was King George V1 who honoured B.-P. with the royal family's highest award, the Order of Merit (no more than 24 holders at any one time).

At B.-P.'s suggestion, St. George, the patron saint of England, was declared the patron saint of Scouting (reputedly this is the day England's famous bard, William Shakespeare, was born and, sweet sorrow, also died).

In 1934 St. George's Chapel, Windsor, became the special place for a national service/parade of British King's Scouts and holders of Scout gallantry awards. Parades are held every year, though B.-P. only ever attended one (in 1937).

B.-P.'s and Olave's memorial tablet in Westminster Abbey is in the St. George's Chapel.

The B.-P. Memorial Fund was launched on St. George's Day 1942.

ST. GEORGE

In 1914 B.-P. had suggested Troops and Districts celebrate St. George's Day as an annual event, but the practice was slow to develop at first, due to the war.

The Movement Post-Baden-Powell

The Scouts, as well as everyone else, suffered from the difficulties of continued rationing and scant resources. For some in the movement there was a hint of going back to the pioneering days of 1908 - uniform was hard to get hold of in the forties, so such things as scarves were made from tea-towels and dyed the appropriate colour. 1947, in addition to being the year that the Boy Scout Association was fortunate enough to acquire part of the lost manuscript of *Scouting for Boys*, also saw the first Jamboree without B.-P.'s presence. The 'Jamboree of Peace', held in France, welcomed Scouts from **70** countries. Olave attended this and all other Jamborees bar one until she died in 1977 (her ashes were buried in her husband's grave in Nyeri). The Jamboree she was unable to attend, she liked to recall, was the only one which suffered a typhoon. It happened to be called Typhoon Olive.

Without its charismatic founder, the movement has never been quite the same, and could never be. He was a person who worked on intuition, who had a host of natural gifts and the ability to inspire just about anyone who came into contact with him, from Wolf Cub to King. Inevitably the movement became a movement governed by committees and increased red tape, with little room for individuals. Although it had some fine and inspirational people working for it, by the 1950s Britain was vastly different to pre-war times. It is doubtful whether B.-P. ever saw a television set in his lifetime, yet the music, language and social habits of society became increasingly influenced by this new powerful medium. Scouting activities, too, could be encountered in schools, through the new Duke of Edinburgh Award scheme, and the burgeoning professional youth service.

Modernisation became a mantra for some of the movement's members though the fifties and sixties still saw the movement having a strong and healthy hold on many of the nation's young boys and (a new term) teenagers. Upon entering the Scout hut, the Scoutmaster ('Skip' now rather than Sir or Mr) would be saluted rather than shaken by the hand. Formal inspections and prayers would be balanced with British Bulldogs and a detour to the chippie on the way home. The array of equipment and gadgets, alluring smell and squeak of leather at the local Scout shop, along with regular hikes and camps still captivated many boys' minds. They were the first generation to be born after the death of the movement's founder - to many young members of the movement B.-P. was now a vaguely remembered name rather than a person.

Naturally the **1957** centenary of B.-P.'s birth and fiftieth anniversary of Scouting would be a momentous occasion for the movement. On the date of B.-P.'s birthday, many members placed and lit a candle in the window of their homes. The major event of the year was the huge Jamboree held in Sutton Coldfield, Birmingham. Campers from Britain and all over the world were housed in the vast canvas city (**970** hectares and a service team totalling **2,700** people). At the time, special postage stamps were released by the GPO, and it was said to have been the BBC's largest ever outside broadcast. In scenes re-enacting B.-P.'s life, his son, Peter, played the part of his father at Mafeking. B.-P. was aged 43 at the time, and his son also happened to be 43 when playing him.

The foundation stone for Baden-Powell House was laid by Olave on the 17th October 1959. Built on a bombed site at 67 Queen's Gate, South Kensington, SW7, the house/hostel was finally opened by the Queen during the **seventh** month of 1961. With **seven** storeys, and easily accessible to all parts of central London, boys could have bed and breakfast for 10/6 a night. Fittingly, it was just minutes from former homes of B.-P.'s. And around the corner was Stanhope Mews - B.-P. had first come in to the world at Stanhope Street. Baden-Powell House was also opposite the Natural History and other famous museums, the first of which had opened in **1857**. (Henrietta's sister had married Sir William Henry Flower, the then Director of the Natural History Museum. Another family link: the work of Charles Darwin, a friend of B.-P.'s father, could/can be explored just across the road from B.-P. House).

Left and below:
Baden-Powell House in
2007 and 1961

The well known statue of B.-P. which stands outside Baden-Powell House, South Kensington, is by artist and sculptor Don Potter. A good friend of B.-P.'s, he lived to be 102; he is seen here adding some final touches. It is said to be London's only granite statue.

It was also in July 1961 that the owner of Brownsea Island, John Bonham Christie (he had been a Scout himself) welcomed fifty Scouts on a visit. The island had become known as the 'Forbidden Island' (or 'Mystery Island') to locals and it had been around thirty years since Scouts had last been allowed to set foot on Brownsea. After the purchase of the island by the National Trust in 1962 (with part of it being leased to the John Lewis Partnership as a leisure outlet), Scouts and Guides were granted privileged camping rights the following year when it was officially opened to the public by Olave Lady Baden-Powell.

Modern-day Brownsea Island

With the best of intentions, the movement, under Chief Scout Sir Charles Maclean's Advance Party Committee, would assess its whole purpose and position in society, and change dramatically. Out went terms such as Boy and Wolf; khaki, shorts and the big hat also vanished along with the pole. But amazingly now, in the 1960s and 1970s it was still perfectly normal for Scouts to be seen walking down the street with knives, often sheath knives, attached to their (now sometimes plastic) Scout belts (as if being armed with wooden poles hadn't been enough!). At this time the number seven, such a significant digit for Baden-Powell, would almost make him turn in his grave (or so some said, including Olave and other family members). Sir Charles Maclean had made D - Day the deadline for publishing his committee's report - 6/6/66 - and all the various changes in uniform, terminology and programme that came after publication of the *Advance Party Report* were phased in from October 1967. It also included the reducing of the 10 original ('sacred' to many) Scout laws to 7. Such huge changes resulted in, it is said, some 25 - 30,000 members leaving the movement (and prompted Olave to donate many of her husband's Scouting items to collections and archives overseas). But the Scouts, no longer 'square' or cissies, braved the storm and eventually increased in numbers and confidence.

Sir Charles 'Chips' Maclean, the 27th Chief of Duart and instigator of the *Advance Party Report* (APR), went down in Scout history as the man who outlawed shorts in 1967, though in fact an option to wear long trousers had been introduced for older Scouts well before the APR, in 1961. Uniform longs were priced at £2.10s - not considered cheap!; the option to wear a beret instead of the big hat had been given even earlier, in 1952.

'Chips' Maclean was also responsible for starting a Cub Pack so that Prince Andrew could enjoy Cub Scouting (his mother had been a Guide after all). Sir Charles did not interfere with the running of the Pack though it really was a **BP** Cub Pack as the meetings were held in Buckingham Palace. On visiting the Pack one day, Sir Charles was asked to tell a yarn. He told them about his ancestral home, Duart Castle. Listening with awe at the castle's gory past, one of the Cubs asked if there was a ghost at the castle. An erudite interjection came from the Royal Cub, "But there's only one ghost, isn't there? The Holy Ghost."

Sir Charles had been a Cub, and when of Cub age he'd actually unwittingly met Scouting's founder whilst on a ferry crossing. Aboard the steamer, a very young Charles Maclean waved enthusiastically to a distant figure stood in Duart Castle, on the Isle of Mull. Slightly puzzled, a retired Lieutenant-General asked him to whom he was waving. The boy, known as 'Chips', answered that it was his grandfather.

The soldier - Baden-Powell - had reached his early fifties, and yet in the early first quarter of the twentieth century he had succeeded in sparking a revolution in youth work for boys. The boy, destined to become the fourth Chief Scout, by the time he'd entered his early fifties, had been the catalyst for another revolution in youth work, only it involved the very same movement.

Left: Chief Scout Sir Charles Maclean was also Chief Scout of the Commonwealth.

Below: 1966, a family snap of two Stevenage Scouts in the soon-to-be old uniform.

"Say what you like—it's practical."

National Headquarters at 25 Buckingham Palace Road, 1917 to 1974

Above: 15th Finchley Scout Group ~ thriving and with the 'modern' uniform

I am sure that B.-P. would be pleased (and slightly envious?) with the present Chief Scout, actor and former **Blue Peter** presenter Peter Duncan. Scouting was really the true Blue Peter before television came along (if writing to the programme, incidentally, the postcode is W12 6**BP**). Not only does Peter Duncan bear the name of B.-P.'s son, Peter Duncan's son, Arthur, shares one of B.-P.'s son's names (the 2nd Lord Baden-Powell was christened Arthur Robert Peter). Peter Duncan, too, has starred in the founder's favourite play *Peter Pan*. (Additionally, B.-P. was married in St. Peter's Church, Dorset, and buried in the grounds of St. Peter's Church, South Africa. For Catholics in other parts of the world, the feast of St. Peter happens to be held on **22nd February**.)

And of the centenary? In 2007 B.-P. might not immediately recognise a Scout. The badges have changed (even the gender sometimes, as the movement is now coeducational), Scouts are not quick to salute, the laws have altered and the only recognisable item of uniform would be the scarf ("What! no hat?" the founder might well enquire). Yet, ironically, in the space of a hundred years, it could be argued that progress has done little to improve the physical, social, mental and spiritual well-being of many young people - particularly their social and spiritual development. Thinking of others, helping others, doing things to improve yourself, concepts such as service, loyalty and duty: all these things still need teaching today. It has taken a hundred years for B.-P.'s important notion of citizenship and character training to fully enter the public domain and be (often tentatively) taught in schools.

B.-P. reflected on the significantly high numbers of young army recruits who had to be turned away through bad teeth and poor fitness during the South African War. He also wanted to do something to deter young lads from wasting their money, drinking and smoking, hanging around on street corners and getting into trouble. In 2007 'loafing', as he called it, hasn't gone away. His concerns about the young loitering, drinking, and smoking are still here today, sadly the problem has escalated into drugs, knives and guns too (it makes the arguments over militarism seem rather hollow and petty now). The lack of personal goals and basic physical fitness among some (not all) of the young has grown into epidemic proportions. The well-being and life chances for many boys, too, need more Baden-Powell figures to come forward and fight their corner.

Strangely, it is often the older and better-off young adults who are enjoying their Scouting, albeit outside the movement. The dawn of a new century has seen an amazing back-to-nature and simple fun revival in Scouting-like activities. The Camping and Caravanning Club has seen a year on year increase in membership from 2000 to 2007. There has also been a proliferation of television programmes by Ray Mears and others on bushcraft and survival; also the Brat Camp, Castaway and Jungle survival programmes where the participants are put into tribes (patrols?) and set challenges. Nature, using and enjoying the environment responsibly, education, citizenship, self-help, helping others, being proud of your country: it was all part of B.-P.'s plan back in 1907 to make 'happy, healthful and helpful citizens'; most of his Scouting ideas are just as important and relevant today as they were 100 years ago.

3rd Bromley Scouts (Kent) in the 1920s and in 2007

(teal green uniform shirts since 2002).

Some Connected Names and Faces

B.-P.'s brother George, the Queen Mother, the Prince of Wales.
Lord Roberts, Chief Dinizulu, Rudyard Kipling.
(Bottom row) 'the Boy' McLaren, Buffalo Bill, B.-P.'s son Peter.

Sir Arthur Pearson was born on the 24th February 1866. He suffered from glaucoma and eventually went blind. He was a friend and adviser to Joseph Chamberlain (English statesman, at one time president of the local government board). Despite being known as a great hustler he was known for numerous 'good-turns', a major one was founding the St. Dunstan's Home for blinded soldiers (the organisation is still in existence today). In his younger days, having heard from a doctor that the best preventive for the ensuing flu epidemic was something obtained from the eucalyptus tree, Pearson arranged to have it sprayed on all his newspapers. In 1921 he died tragically in his bath after slipping and falling unconscious. On his passing, Lord Northcliffe, owner of *The Times,* commented: *I have known him since 1884 - a strange, erratic and in some ways noble character. He is in my mind today of course.*

John Hassall (1868 - 1948) designed the front covers of *Scouting for Boys*, he also undertook other occasional tasks for the BSA, including designing the front cover of the movement's first leaders' magazine, the *Headquarters Gazette.* The son of a naval officer (who died when Hassall was still a young boy), he twice failed entry to Sandhurst, and emigrated briefly to Canada to study farming. He promptly studied art abroad and married in 1893, soon becoming a well known illustrator and designer of posters/advertisements for a wide range of products, from a programme for the play *Peter Pan*, to: Lipton's Jellies, HP Sauce, Cooper's Sheep Dip and Biscuit Boy. With the hardships of old age, his sight deteriorated and he became less active.

Charles van Raalte (1857 - 1907) was born in Lancashire. He married in 1887 and purchased Brownsea Island in 1901. In 1902 he became Mayor of Poole. He previously resided at the family estate of Aldenham Abbey, Hertfordshire. His father Marcus was a wealthy stockbroker, and Charles followed suit by dealing in tobacco and Jute. He was a JP, Freemason, and became Vice-President of Poole Conservative Club. A well known and popular local figure, upon his death, flags were flown at half-mast. The will recorded Charles van Raalte's gross value as £380,331. He left the island to his widow, and £100 to each servant of six years' service.

LADY BADEN-POWELL, GBE ~
A POTTED BIOGRAPHY

Shock! The age difference between B.-P. and his wife Olave St Clair Soames, was large. When they got married she was 23 and he was 55 (though at that time the age difference wouldn't have been considered particularly unusual). Some Boy Scouts, at first, were not impressed with their founder's 'disloyalty' to them and the new movement. They were soon won over, however, by B.-P.'s wife.

Born in Chesterfield in 1889 to Katharine and Harold Soames, Olave shared her birthday (22nd February) with the campaigning soldier she would eventually marry. She grew up without attending any formal school or taking exams. Her brother Arthur's son (Olave's nephew) married Mary, daughter of Sir Winston Churchill.

Although B.-P.'s wife was born into a well-to-do family, as a girl Olave considered herself to be the dunce of the family and was something of a tomboy. Her father, in anticipation of a much wanted boy, had planned to call 'him' by the old Danish name of Olaf. Olaf (pronounced Olev) became Olave. She thought nothing of sliding down banisters or taking the tin baths outside. Here she would indulge in playing 'bath-polo' on the lake with her friend. Whilst a keen and competent violinist, she also had tremendous stamina and was amazingly sporty. In addition to swimming and ratting, she enjoyed all racket games, billiards, skating, hockey and riding both bicycles and horses. She could play many sets of tennis and sometimes played friendly matches with Miss Bromfield, a Wimbledon Lawn Tennis Championship competitor.

Olave used to play on railway tracks! For laying pennies on the railway tracks near Bradfield, Devon she was hauled before the Chief Inspector. Actually she got off with a friendly caution; the inspector was a G.W.R. man at Tiverton Junction. As Olave explains in her autobiography, the pleasurable occupation entailed: *lying low and waiting to see how much they were flattened when a train went over them. We used to put a pin on each penny and it flattened into a little sword. It was a stupid thing to do, for I suppose we could even have derailed a train.*

As soon as they were married, Olave swiftly put all her energy into assisting her husband with the movement. She even became a Lady Scoutmaster of the local Ewhurst Troop. Within a very short period, however, she rose through the ranks of the Girl Guide movement, becoming Guide Commissioner for Sussex and, by 1918, Chief Guide. It is no secret that there was no love lost between Agnes, B.-P.'s sister and Olave. Along with B.-P., Agnes was the founder of the Girl Guides, and became the Guides' first President but

Olave went on to become World Chief Guide. Even with her own children, Peter, Heather and Betty, Olave did not consider herself to be a natural doting mother. Her husband and the two movements came first.

After B.-P.'s death, Olave was given by King George V a grace and favour apartment in Hampton Court Palace. She lived out almost all the remaining years of her life at Hampton Court, though a few years before her death she moved to a nursing home near Guildford. It was here, weak and suffering from diabetes that she eventually passed away on 25th June 1977.

Left: Tomboy? and (bottom left) age 21

All complete: the B.-P. family

BADEN-POWELL'S CONNECTIONS
AND CONTEMPORARIES

Baden-Powell was contemporary/nearly contemporary with: Rudyard Kipling, 1865; Sir James Barrie, 1860; Kenneth Grahame, 1859; Sir Arthur Conan Doyle, 1859; Sir Arthur Pearson, 1866; Cecil Rhodes, 1853; Sir William Smith (founder of the Boys' Brigade), 1854; Ernest Thompson Seton, 1860; H. G. Wells, 1866; Joseph Conrad, 1857; Sir Edward Elgar, 1857; Daniel Beard, 1850.

B.-P. knew, met and/or corresponded with many famous people, including: members of the royal family at home and abroad, prime ministers, presidents, Annie Besant, Thomas Hardy, Cecil Rhodes, Rudyard Kipling, Sir Winston Churchill, Guglielmo Marconi, Browning, Lord Meath, Buffalo Bill, Mussolini, Sir Arthur Conan Doyle, Lord Kitchener, Tsar Nicholas 11 (his son was a Scout), Sir Ernest Shackleton, Pope Pius X1.

B.-P.'s mother also met many influential people, particularly with her husband's connections. In addition to meeting scientists such as Sir John Herschel and William Fox Talbot, and writers/poets such as Thackeray and Browning, Henrietta came into contact with Ruskin and consulted him on her son's ambidextrous drawing.

BADEN-POWELL:
DID YOU KNOW?

In 1929 B.-P. was offered a peerage for his work for the movement, though he wasn't going to pay for the honour! Although normally costing more than a thousand pounds for the privilege, in the case of B.-P., after a bout of letter writing by his staff and press secretary, the usual fee was waived. He became Lord Baden-Powell of Gilwell.

~~~~~~~~~

Baden-Powell's wife, Olave, turned to spiritualism after her husband's death. It is said that mediums reported to her that her late husband had had conversations with King George V1 and even with Christ.

~~~~~~~~~

With his *Scouting for Boys*, Baden-Powell became one of the most widely-read British authors of all time. From the first edition of 1908, until his death, he wrote a piece in practically every edition of *The Scout* paper. He also wrote regular articles for magazines and newspapers, including the *Daily Mail*.

~~~~~~~~~

Members of B.-P.'s family had little chance of being aloof from the Scout movement. His sister helped to found the Girl Guides, and, soon after, his wife married the 'Scout man' and his movement. Two of B.-P.'s brothers also took on duties. Warington advised on Sea Scout matters and wrote the Sea Scouts' handbook, whilst Baden Fletcher was President of both South West London Scout District and North London District. Baden looked very much like his famous brother. An expert balloonist (B.-P. appointed him Commissioner for Aviation) and also a member of the Inner Magic Circle, after the Great War he became DC for Sevenoaks Scout District, keeping that appointment until his death seventeen years later.

~~~~~~~~~

B.-P. was ambidextrous though his daughter Betty remembered him usually preferring the right hand when using a pencil, and the left for using a pen.

~~~~~~~~~

Although B.-P. received much fan mail and far too many invitations from around the world, he wasn't without occasional criticism. He once received in the post a small model of a black coffin, in it was a note telling him he should bury the Scout movement.

~~~~~~~~~

When B.-P. was at the BSA offices attending meetings, he was known to be always doodling: one hand working on an outline of a sketch while the other adding some shading.

Apparently there was always a rush afterwards by the office boys for the Chief's blotting paper.

~~~~~~~~~~

Baden Powell was a yawl which hailed from King's Lynn. Built for the sum of £60.00 in 1901, the sturdy Baden Powell was used by its owners mainly to catch shrimp, cockles and mussels (it is still in existence today). Many roads, schools and other institutions carry the founder's name (even boys born after the Mafeking success were christened Baden Powell).

~~~~~~~~~~

Baden-Powell was not the only soldier to write a book on scouting. R. Donajowski of the Kings Own Regiment published *A Soldier's Aid to Scouting* in 1898.

~~~~~~~~~~

Baden Powell was still very much alive and kicking until the year 2000! Born in 1937, although less well known in this country, Baden Powell, the famous acoustic guitarist and composer from Brazil was named after Scouting's founder. This was because his father greatly admired Lord Baden-Powell and the Scout movement.

~~~~~~~~~~

Rose Hill, the Tunbridge Wells preparatory school Baden-Powell attended, is also where his father went to school. Although it has been traditionally said that B.-P. first honed his scouting skills whilst at Charterhouse (sometimes while he should have been in lessons), he wrote to Rose Hill in later life and said that he first developed his scouting and woodcraft skills in the rural setting of the school.

Rose Hill still has Cubs and Brownies today. They enjoy an annual tradition of being given a free ice-cream on Baden-Powell's birthday.

~~~~~~~~~~

When B.-P. died, a grave in the central aisle of the nave of Westminster Abbey had been arranged, but Olave refused this as she considered the Abbey gloomy.

~~~~~~~~~~

Baden-Powell became a member of the London Sketch Club - he was their first 'Guest of the Evening' (and was grateful for their no speeches rule). Although there was absolute silence when sketching, the club could be quite anarchic, with members often dressing up and playing practical jokes: right up B.-P.'s street! We get a flavour of the club when B.-P.'s former Commander in Chief visited. The famous and eminent Lord Roberts might have had his doubts, or at least his footman did according to a book by David Cuppleditch. John Hassall was dressed in a policeman's uniform and waited on the rickety stairs to the club's entrance:

"The lighting arrangements were inadequate and altogether the entrance looked very disreputable, more like the approach to an opium den or gambling hell than respectable club premises," recalled Cecil Aldin. Hassall's presence on the stairs was meant to reassure the guests. He was highly amused at the expression on the face of Lord Roberts' footman, who followed his master up to the first landing. Hassall could not contain his laughter at the man's obvious disgust and, after Lord Roberts had gone inside, our bogus policeman spent some time reassuring the suspicious footman that the General was quite safe. The servant was not fully convinced and remained outside the door until a smiling master reappeared.

In 1958 Cecil B. De Mille, co-founder of Paramount Films, intended to make a film based on the life of Baden-Powell. David Niven was to have had the leading role. The American film director died the following year and the film was never made (though other interested parties kept the idea alive for some time).

Contrary to popular belief, it wasn't Lord Baden-Powell who started the Scout movement in 1907/8. Not technically! It was actually started by Lieutenant-General Baden-Powell (he was neither a Sir nor a Lord).

You can still meet B.-P. today, he's standing in Madame Tussaud's. Alright, you can't talk to him but you might one day get the chance to talk to another real life Lord Baden-Powell: his grandson. The current Lord Baden-Powell is Vice-President of The Scout Association. In 1968, incidentally, Madame Tussaud's were commissioned by the Boy Scouts of America to make a wax effigy of B.-P. to be used in the Johnston Historical Museum. This was said to be the first time one of Tussaud's models had been exported for permanent display overseas.

B.-P.'s favourite words and expressions ~ *Good camping to you all; jolly; ass; My wig!; loafing; sleeves up!; happy, healthful citizens.*

B.-P.'s brother Baden was an expert on military observation balloons and was known in the family as the 'balloonatic'. In 1886 he and B.-P. went in a private capacity to attend the German and Russian manoeuvres; B.-P. landed up getting arrested for spying.

Upon receiving birthday greetings from the 12th East Ham Scout Troop, B.-P. sent the following acknowledgement in 1932:

To writers from every latitude may I say that it's not a mere platitude but a sign of what's really our attitude when we offer our whole hearted gratitude for the greeting you've sent us today.

He practised what he preached, including rising at 5.00am each day
and doing his daily stretches and exercises!

In 1903 Baden-Powell could be bought by the wealthy for approximately £3.00. He appeared in the form of a doll as part of the craze for doll portraiture of famous people that swept through the upper-classes.

~~~~~~~~~~

Baden-Powell received a letter from the Archbishop of Canterbury in 1926 complaining of the movement holding a Rover Scout event over the festival of Easter. A 'Rover Moot' had been organised at the Albert Hall and went ahead.

~~~~~~~~~~

Baden-Powell liked to sleep out in the open, or at least with the windows open when inside. He had the habit of sleeping on his balcony and keeping his feet outside the bedclothes when sleeping.

~~~~~~~~~~

Baden-Powell's eldest brother, Warington, was a keen sailor who patented and designed canoes. In his younger days, as a cadet aboard HMS *Conway*, Warington trained alongside Matthew Webb, who later became the first man to swim the Channel. Warington eventually became a KC in the Admiralty Courts.

~~~~~~~~~~

Baden-Powell's father was a well known scientist and clergyman. Unorthodox for the time, Professor Powell was said to *'have the Sabbath on the brain'*; he remarked on the insufficiency of scriptural grounds for transforming the Jewish Sabbath into the Christian Sunday. He told his wife, Henrietta, that *'every miracle would be explained by natural means in time ... Mesmerism has actually cured the blind and made water taste like wine.'*

~~~~~~~~~~

Neither Baden-Powell nor his wife, Olave, learnt to swim until aged around fifteen.

~~~~~~~~~~

B.-P.'s CV of skills is quite impressive, in addition to playing the ocarina and being an expert Scout/backwoodsman, he was an artist and sculptor (for example, he exhibited a bust of John Smith in the Royal Academy in 1907, and exhibited 125 drawings at the Bruton Gallery). Additionally, he played the piano, and was an actor, horseman, polo player, singer, swordsman, naturalist, comedian, author, educationist...

~~~~~~~~~~

Baden-Powell's family home for many years was Pax Hill, in the village of Bentley, Hampshire. Originally named Blackacre Farm, the Baden-Powells renamed it Pax Hill - 'the hill of peace' - as they'd discovered it during the first week of Peace after the Armistice. They stumbled upon it by pure chance. Having put their bikes on the train to

Farnham, they stopped at the end of a fruitless day's searching to have their sandwiches. And there was the house, at the end of a long rising drive, that caught their eye. Many years later, upon retiring to Kenya, they would name their bungalow Paxtu: Pax being their second Pax, and Tu, apart from punning with two, in Swahili meaning: altogether, complete. In Kenya they had complete peace. Frank Williams, one time District Commissioner in the Allerton area, incidentally, after receiving permission named his own home Pax Hill.

~~~~~~~~

Baden-Powell quote ~ *First I had an idea, then I saw an ideal: now we have a movement and if some of you don't watch out, we shall end up with just an organisation.*

~~~~~~~~

An anagram of Baden-Powell is: *well done bap,* **or** *we all done BP.*

~~~~~~~~

A contemporary and colleague of Charles Darwin, Professor Powell, B.-P.'s father, ill and with his life shortly to expire, was reported to the Bishop of London for heretical preaching.

~~~~~~~~

'He possessed no special disposition for mischief or adventure' wrote B.-P.'s mother about her son as a very young boy.

~~~~~~~~

In 1894, whilst on manoeuvres in Berkshire, England, as Brigade-Major he appeared in the field carrying his right arm in a sling. Having been bitten by a dog, to prevent possible Rabies, his treatment entailed the wearing of a sling and dipping his hand in boiling water several times a day. Riding and working without fuss, with a spirit-lamp and enamelled saucepan he continued this daily 'cure' for the three weeks' duration of the manoeuvres.

~~~~~~~~

Although he rose to achieve high status and was bestowed many accolades, B.-P. was once just a warden! Nothing to do with camping, and not so lowly as it might first appear. B.-P. was Warden of the ancient Livery Company, Mercers' Hall, in the City of London (a family tradition to this day, his father, for example, had been a member too). Incorporated by Royal Charter in 1394, the Company was formed by a collection of merchants to protect their interests, which were primarily the exporting of woollen materials and the importing of luxury fabrics such as silk, linen and cloth of gold. In B.-P.'s time and today the Company had taken on the dual roles of corporate and charitable business (for example establishing Housing Associations and making educational grants). Another, much earlier apprentice and, later, Master of the Company, is Dick Whittington.

~~~~~~~~

Contemporary Baden-Powell family facts: Rosa Baden-Powell, a barrister, became one of television's Master Chef winners in 2001 (she is related to B.-P.'s brother George). A little earlier, in 1993, family member Edward James Baden-Powell played in a rock band that was a support group to Prince at Wembley. There are also twenty-five Baden-Powells recorded in the Australian telephone directory, only nine of whom, however, are directly from B.-P.'s family.

~~~~~~

BADEN-POWELL: A MAN OF MANY NAMES!

Although Scouting's founder was affectionately known as 'B.-P.', to other people during different stages in his life he was well known under other names (and the hyphenation of Baden to Powell didn't occur until B.-P. was aged twelve). As a child he was known to the family as Ste or Stephe (pronounced 'Steevie'). Two of his names, Robert Stephenson, were in honour of the famous engineer's son (who became his godfather but died when Stephe was aged two). At Charterhouse his friends (though he was not known to have close friends) nicknamed him 'Bathing-Towel' or, occasionally, 'Bowel' or 'Guts'. He also acquired the names 'Baking-Powder' and, through his prowess at polo, 'Baden-Polo'. To his very close army friend, Kenneth 'the Boy' McLaren, he was known as James. His African nickname was 'M'hlalapanzi', which meant 'the man who lies down to shoot'. He also acquired the name Impeeza, meaning 'the wolf who never sleeps'. Lastly, Olave, his wife, often called him 'Bin' (short for Robin) or 'Dindo,' her shortened version of 'darling'.

When he started the Scout movement he was originally known as either Colonel or General Baden-Powell (officially he was a Lieutenant-General), but this was superseded by Sir Robert Baden-Powell and, later (also by Scouts today), Lord Baden-Powell of Gilwell. After his death he was often affectionately referred to as 'the old Chief'.

To those unsure in how to pronounce his surname, B.-P. wrote a short verse which he was happy to recite: *Man, Nation, Maiden Please call it Baden. Further, for Powell Rhyme it with Noel.*

B.-P.'S MAIN TITLES (Space does not permit mentioning <u>all</u> of the many decorations and awards conferred on Baden-Powell inside and outside of Britain): 1907, promoted to Lieutenant-General; 1909, knighted;1920, acclaimed Chief Scout of the World; 1922, Baronetcy; 1929, Peerage: Barony - Lord Baden-Powell of Gilwell. In 1937, he was awarded the Wateler Peace Prize. Upon receiving the Order of Merit in the same year, he commented to a Wolf Cub: *'This was won by you and me, but the King presented it to me.'*

FREEDOM OF THE CITY IN: Newcastle on Tyne, Bangor, Cardiff, Harwich, Kingston on Thames (all 1903); Guildford (1928), Poole (1929), Blandford (1929), London (1929), Canterbury (1930), Pontefract (1933).

Above: B.-P. at his Hampshire home ~ Pax Hill

Above: Today it is a nursing home

BADEN-POWELL: WHAT THEY REMEMBERED, SAID OR WROTE ABOUT HIM

More than half a century after his death, writers have commented on the fact that Baden-Powell suffered from an arrested development and had many fears and obsessions. Indeed, others have said that behind the fun-loving old soldier lay a complex and troubled personality. He was a repressed homosexual with latent sadistic tendencies. Or at least that is what a tiny clique of historians and makers of sensationalist documentaries would have you believe! Channel 4's *Secret Lives* series (1995) dug deep in its search for a negative and alternative portrayal of outstanding figures in history. Baden-Powell was one of several weekly victims to receive a highly skewed analysis of their lives.

Needless to say, one cannot really apply twenty-first century experiences, beliefs and mores to a distant and highly unusual personality born and brought up in the Victorian period. The Scout Association's response is, quite rightly, to celebrate the founder's enormous accomplishments rather than trying to assess his personal sex life (ironically, perhaps it is people of the twenty-first century who suffer more than ever before from obsessions and emotional problems, particularly those of a sexual nature). The Scout Association said at the time: *The programme appears to dismiss the tremendous legacy that Baden-Powell left. Anyone whose idea has 25 million subscribers throughout the world must have got something right.*

Historian Tim Jeal, on the other hand, reminds us that without being the 'boy-man' and without his unique family, school and social experiences Baden-Powell could not have dreamt up his humble though globally successful scheme for boys. Another historian, Michael Rosenthal, no lover of the founder of the world's largest voluntary youth movement, wrote: .... *Baden-Powell must be judged one of the most prolific and successful popular writers of the twentieth century.*

What follows are observations and personal insights from people of all ages, from the well known to the every-day mortal, who came into contact with B.-P. We have, in other words, formal and informal memories that help us move away from the famous heroic colonel once studied by dry historians, depicted on cigarette cards or profiled in schoolboys' books and annuals.

~~~~~~~~~

On his death, Nurse Mrs. Cranwick, who had been in Mafeking Hospital during the siege of Mafeking, remarked: *I always found him fair, just and a staunch disciplinarian.*

~~~~~~~~~

Sir Humphrey Noble, who attended B.-P.'s Brownsea Island camp with his brother, had met Scouting's founder on numerous occasions at his grandfather's home. He recalled in *The Scouter* of July 1957:

....he was a most charming, amusing, interesting and talented guest, a "good mixer" as we say now, and a fine amateur actor. Gilbert and Sullivan operas and plays were often done when he came to stay: consequently he knew all the family very well.

Boy Scouts at rallies often remarked, later on, on noticing the shiny coat of B.-P.'s horse, and the founder's tanned and weather-beaten complexion. A. A. Dowle recalled in a letter a similar experience:

One of the highlights of my Scouting career in the late twenties was meeting Lord Baden-Powell off a Union Castle ship at berth 36 in Southampton Docks early one Monday morning on his return from a visit to South Africa. He shook our left hands, which some of us were reluctant to wash afterwards! With the quaintness memory plays on one, I can clearly recall noting how wrinkled his brown knees were.

Major A.G. Wade, a family friend and husband of B.-P.'s long-serving personal secretary, Eileen Wade, lived close to B.-P. in the village of Bentley, Hampshire. In an article for *Country Life* he wrote of B.-P.'s community spirit, for example at Christmas time:

Christmas was an anxious time for B.-P. He had a nightmare lest some child in Bentley should be forgotten and go to bed on Christmas Night without having had a toy. And so, after tea on Christmas Day he used to come to me and we would go round the cottages where there were children. With him he brought large sacks of surplus toys from Pax, [the B.-P.s' home] and outside the cottage doors we used to leave a bundle, knocking on the door before we left. He never showed himself on these occasions; the knock was to make sure that the presents would be taken in.

It was also mentioned in the same article how B.-P. avoided one of the numerous impromptu visits paid to his residence:

I remember an occasion when, dressed as he generally was in very elderly clothes, some strangers coming up the drive mistook him for the gardener and enquired if Lord Baden-Powell was at home. Sizing up those particular visitors, B.-P. accepted the role and, truthfully enough, replied that he was afraid he was out.

From *Country Life*, January 18th 1941

A slight, reddish, freckled, not very tall Edwardian gentleman.

Rex Hazlewood describing B.-P. in the *Diamond Jubilee Book of Scouting*, 1966.

~~~~~~~~

But for that generalship of which Baden-Powell was a master, the Boy Scout movement might have led to the defiant experiments characteristic of German youth: as it was, under his leadership it became orderly, constitutional and imperialist and, as Gilbert Armitage wrote,

> *'the roar heard in Mafeking*
> *is muted to a pious wheeze*
> *of sound advice on life and string*
> *to little brats with naked knees.'*

... The Scout movement was the very breath of hope and love and encouragement to many a child. In the decade from 1908 to 1918 no other influence upon British boyhood came anywhere near it.

From Leslie Paul, author of *Angry Young Man*. A pacifist, as a young adult he founded his own youth movement.

~~~~~~~~

... a wonderful man, not at all pompous but relaxed and jovial, a gifted speaker with a terrific personality, friendly to all and very approachable.

Don Potter, a life-long Scouting friend. Among his many fine works, Don sculpted the Brownsea Island commemorative stone erected to remember B.-P.'s experimental camp.

~~~~~~~~

Both the Chief and Lady Baden-Powell had the wonderful gift of making one feel at home. Once, at a dinner in the Hall of the Mercer's Company of which he was at one time Master, I was sitting at a table some feet away from the top table where he was chief guest. Suddenly I heard his familiar voice, "Hallo, ugly!". It may sound a doubtful compliment but it made my evening.

Claude Fisher, at that time a young member of HQ staff.

~~~~~~~~

More than any of Britain's contributions to shaping contemporary Youth, it was Baden-Powell who revolutionised the process of growing up. He may have been a limited old buffer, and all good wishes to his successors who are trying to make his movement less Philistine and less, in the bad sense, boyish; but even his most grudging admirers must admit that he was an improvement on witch doctors and tribal elders as a programmer of boys' spare time. How relaxed and humane the Scouts seem compared to paramilitary youth movements: nobody has ever huddled under the sheets because They are coming.

Punch magazine July 1966

~~~~~~~~~~~

P. B. Nevill OBE, a well known and important Commissioner in the movement, knew B.-P. well. In one of his books Nevill describes staying at the Chief's home for a week:

It was always a great experience to stay with the Chief and Lady B.-P. For one thing you could always be sure that you would be kept busy! If you wanted to have a quiet chat with him, the plan was to get up at 5.30 a.m., for at that time it would be his custom to go out for a walk with his dogs. If you missed this there was not much opportunity during the day. After breakfast he would retire to his study to deal with his correspondence and the hundred and one things he always had on hand, while the visitors would be set to work in the garden. At lunch he would appear, probably with a number of papers, and quite likely you would find yourself with one or more of these in your hands, with a request to peruse and let him have your opinion thereon at tea time. B.-P. had a wonderful knack of getting other people to work for him. You felt it an honour that he should ask you to help, and consequently you did your best. This is one of the reasons, I am sure, why he accomplished so much.

~~~~~~~~~~~

Enid Marsh is the daughter of Stanley Ince OBE, an early warden of the Roland House Scout hostel that once existed in Stepney, east London. Ince was a friend of B.-P.'s, and B.-P. became unofficial god-father to Ince's daughter. Enid remembers being afraid to kiss B.-P. because of his prickly moustache. Although a child at the time, she also recalls:

I just knew he was an important person but he just treated me as though he were an uncle. At Scout events he had a commanding presence ... I was on the Adriatic cruise with him and Olave during the 1930s. By this time he was quite ill and slowing up. He never got off board or mixed company. Olave performed all the formal duties.

~~~~~~~~~~~

Sir Percy Everett, author of *The First Ten Years,* wrote in the final sentence to his introduction:

To him I owe 40 years of supreme happiness.

~~~~~~~~~~~

Tim Jeal remarks that B.-P.'s son-in-law, Gervas, found his future father-in-law a daunting proposition because of his age and fame. He goes on:

When offered a glass of flat beer at luncheon, dare he ask for a fresh bottle? And was Baden-Powell serious about wanting him to bring a gun on his next visit so that he could shoot a rabbit which had been destroying the lawn? He brought the gun, but was tormented by fears of missing the animal or earning the great man's displeasure by shooting it while sitting. But when the Chief Scout roared: "There he is!" Gervas shot the sitting rabbit and earned nothing but praise. Given Baden-Powell's saintly public reputation, Gervas was surprised to learn that Olave disliked being driven by her husband since he swore so much. He was also disconcerted to discover that Baden-Powell did not shake hands with a firm grip; and worse than that, that the hero of Mafeking's hands were soft and rather puffy in spite of his vigorous morning exercises.

~~~~~~~~~~

G. Chilton, a Scout Commissioner in Marlborough, recalled that Laurie, a Wolf Cub, was desperately ill in Savernake Hospital:

The County Commissioner, Dr. Walter Maurice, despaired of Laurie's recovery. Meeting the General Secretary of the Scout movement one day Dr. Maurice asked him to get the Chief (B.-P.) to write a letter to Laurie. B.-P. apparently wrote him a charming letter, which the boy's mother framed and put above his bed. From that moment Laurie began to get better, and grew to be a fit man working for British Railways.

~~~~~~~~~~

In a history of the 30th Reigate Scout Group (1925 - 2000), the editor, Steve Robinson records someone else sleeping in B.-P.'s bed!

During the 2nd World War the Rev. H. J. Anderson (former SM of the 4th Reigate Troop) had been billeted at Pax Hill, B.-P.'s former home. He was pleased to find that he'd been given B.-P.'s own bedroom. The Officer apologised for being able only to offer B.-P.'s own bed, saying "When you wake up, that is if you get to sleep on it, you'll think you're dead and have been laid on a slab!". He did find it a bit uncomfortable, but was thrilled by the experience.

~~~~~~~~~~

John Hargrave had been appointed Commissioner for Camping and Woodcraft by B.-P. He later left the movement to start the Socialist/pacifist Kibbo Kift youth movement. He wrote of B.-P. as being a 'mental psychic', going on to say:

There was a Huck Finn hidden in Baden-Powell - a kind of backwoods' urchin, or maybe gremlin - that tugged pretty hard and might easily have upset the whole jamboree ... It broke loose in small exuberances and tricksy quirks ... It was the Boy-Poltergeist in Baden-Powell - that made rapport with the primitive fraternity gang spirit of boyhood. Like a true poltergeist it rang a bell and rapped on the door ... And thousands of boys ... ran after it to camp. They made their escape from a dreary, half-dead commercialised and deadly dull civilization, and during the weekends anyhow pretended to be backwoodsmen ... Baden-Powell tapped the primitive urge that is cribb'd, cabin'd and confined by civilized herd-conditioning and convention. He tapped it and unlocked it. And for a while ... it ran free.

~~~~~~~~~

My first meeting with the Chief Scout was in 1913. Wishing to see him on business I called at Headquarters, where a Secretary, smoking a pipe, and an Assistant-Secretary, also smoking a pipe, held me in converse till the Chief was at liberty. Both were very busy, and extremely polite. Anxious to "Be prepared," I inquired of the Secretary - judiciously, of course - what demeanour one ought to adopt in meeting his principal.

*"Never ask the Chief," said he, "how you shall do a thing; **do it**! He will forgive a mistake, and he loves a 'trier.'"*

A very shrewd observation, Mr. Secretary, as I have since discovered.

I was a little disconcerted at this particular interview by noticing that all the time I talked B.-P. was sketching the most hideous faces on his blotting-pad with his left hand. "If those faces have any relation to his thoughts," I reflected, "the sooner I clear out the better." I had no cause for alarm. He understood my proposition perfectly, and our business was concluded with a laugh and a handshake that sent me away happy.

A contributor writing in the London Scouts' magazine *The Trail* in April 1918.

~~~~~~~~~

Mountaineer and social reformer, Sir John Hunt, led the first successful expedition to climb Mount Everest. In 1956 he became director of the Duke of Edinburgh's Award Scheme. The extract below is taken from *Jubilee Journal* 5th August 1957, published in both English and French.

SALUTE TO B.-P.
BY SIR JOHN HUNT, C.B.E., D.S.O., D.C.L.,LL.D.

Every once in a while there appears upon the stage of life some person who, by a sure and seemingly magic touch, appeals successfully to the deepest feelings and finest qualities within the rest of mankind and inspires them to reach beyond themselves. This is convincing testimony of inspired leadership; it is the greater if the effects of such dynamism endure to touch the lives of many people after that leader has passed on. If there is also in that same person the quality of humility, then you have a man or a woman who numbers among the truly great.

Baden-Powell was such a man. Those who, unlike myself, had the fortune to know him, will need no persuading of this fact. But for countless others, we have the evidence of his achievement. For this man has been the means of placing on the path of full and happy living millions of men and women, who have graduated to citizenship through Scouting and Guiding - given them a way of life based on giving rather than getting, on always doing their best.

To-day we need to widen the bounds of Scouting and Guiding, to wake the spirit of Baden-Powell in many more boys and girls, if we are to enable to-morrow's citizens to develop the qualities of selflessness, self-reliance, enterprise and the vision of world brotherhood, which they will need to safeguard the future. This does not, necessarily mean that many more boys and girls must become Scouts and Guides; it does mean that Scouts and Guides must look increasingly beyond their movement in interpreting the message of Baden-Powell.

~~~~~~~~~

Betty Clay CBE, B.-P.'s youngest daughter, when contributing to the book *Growing up in the Twenties*, wrote of her father:

He was marvellous as a father: he was so amusing, so loving. I can't imagine anyone being a more solicitous, thoughtful and devoted father than he was. He was absolutely wonderful - kept us always in great amusement and laughter. He was full of jokes and fun.

~~~~~~~~~

EXTRACTS FROM SIR WINSTON CHURCHILL'S BOOK *GREAT CONTEMPORARIES* (1938, where he lists three Generals he held in high esteem: Generals Booth, Botha and Baden-Powell)

I remember well the first time I saw the hero of this article, now Lord Baden-Powell. I had gone with my regimental team to play in the Cavalry Cup at Meerut. There was a great gathering of the sporting and social circles of the British Army in India. In the evening an amateur vaudeville entertainment was given to a large company. The feature of this was a sprightly song and dance by an officer of the garrison, attired in the brilliant uniform of an Austrian Hussar, and an attractive lady. Sitting as a young lieutenant in the stalls, I was struck by the quality of the performance, which certainly would have held its own on the boards of any of our music-halls. I was told:

"That's B.-P. An amazing man! He won the Kader Cup, has seen lots of active service. They think no end of him as a rising soldier; but fancy a senior officer kicking his legs up like that before a lot of subalterns!"

I was fortunate in making the acquaintance of this versatile celebrity before the polo tournament was over.

...One wondered why B.-P. seemed to drop out of the military hierarchy after the South African War was over. He held distinguished minor appointments but ... There is no doubt Whitehall resented the disproportionate acclamation which the masses had bestowed upon a single figure ... At any rate, the bright fruition of fortune and success was soon obscured by a chilly fog through which indeed the sun still shone, but with a dim and baffled ray.

~~~~~~~~~~

Former Scout Commissioner Jack Kellam, interviewed by the author in September 1998, aged 98, remembered B.-P. as follows:

Sir Robert had an imposing presence, while his voice had remarkable carrying power. It was surprising to find that, at rallies, when he was addressing the boys from the centre of the ground hardly a word of what he said was lost to those in the press box, a hundred yards or more away.

B.-P. was tremendous. If he walked into the coffee room at HQ Scout Club, everyone would stand up. You could feel him almost before you saw him.

~~~~~~~~~~

Sir Peter Scott, son of the great Antarctic explorer Captain Robert Scott, had Sir James Barrie as a godfather. Barrie, of course, was author of B.-P.'s favourite play *Peter Pan*. The very young Peter Scott's mother was influenced by B.-P. on one occasion, he tells us in his autobiography:

I must have been quite young when my mother found herself sitting one night at a dinner next to Lord Baden-Powell, the Chief Scout. He was ambidextrous and showed her the advantages of being able to write and draw with both hands. It would be nice, she thought, if her son, too, was ambidextrous; so from then onwards she started taking the pencil out of my right hand when I was drawing and putting it into my left. This might have achieved what she intended had she not slightly overdone it, so that I have been left-handed ever since. That is the story she used to tell, although privately I think I might have been left-handed anyway.

~~~~~~~~~~

Andrew Paterson was an employee of Pearson's, publishers of Boy Scout material. He was there in 1908 when it all started. Writing in *The Scouter* of July 1957 he recalled:

Like most of the younger generation of fifty years ago, I regarded him with feelings of awe and admiration. Was he not the outstanding hero of the recent Boer War?

But after a few months, during which time I had the opportunity to see him more or less closely, I began to be puzzled and in fact began to wonder how a man of his temperament should have become associated with a movement for young people. He was not young - he had turned fifty - and fifty seems old age to boys. He was unmarried, and bachelors, as a rule, are staid in their ways and have little use for youngsters. And he was one who had attained high rank in the army, which meant that he was accustomed to barking out orders and expected to have them instantly obeyed, a characteristic that tended to make him seem brusque and stand-offish to the young. And yet it was this man with all these handicaps, so to speak, who was divinely chosen - and I use the word divinely deliberately - to head the Boy Scout Movement.

Frank Dawes, author of a book on the Boys' Club movement titled *A Cry from the Streets*, showed objectivity when he wrote:

Baden-Powell was not, however, a simple soldier or an unpractical dreamer. He was a brilliant man of many parts - an actor, writer, artist and humorist, a sailor and horseman, and above all an educationist with a great understanding of the needs of boyhood and youth. He saw that the new education intent, as Trevelyan says, "on producing not peasants but clerks," inculcated ambition to win prizes and secure pay and position instead of the old-fashioned public school values of commonsense, manners, guts and, above all, service for others. To him, in the 1920s, it came as no surprise that the country was divided against itself with self-seeking individuals, cliques, political parties, religious sects and social classes. Like most upper class men of his time he was intensely patriotic and he aimed to strengthen national unity by bringing up boys who were efficient morally and physically, with the idea of using that efficiency in the service of the community as a whole. He saw more clearly than most that the great towns in which most of the nation lived had robbed boys of their heritage of field and hedgerow, green valley and hill, woods and streams. By giving the heritage back to succeeding generations of boys, he ensured that his name would live when boys had forgotten who was the hero of Mafeking.

Salute to B.-P. By The Rt. Hon. Harold Wilson OBE, MP.

I am glad to have this opportunity as a former Cub, King's Scout and Rover - and the father of a Scout and Cub - to join in the tributes that are being paid at this time to the memory of B.-P. and for all that he did for the youth of the world by founding, and for over thirty years, guiding the Scout movement.

My generation was lucky enough to know B.-P. and to be able to see him at Jamborees and local rallies, as well as to read his inspiring and entertaining weekly articles in The Scout. During his lifetime the Scout movement - in Britain and all over the free world - progressed and developed in a way he could never have dreamed of when he embarked on his historic experiment at Brownsea Island.

Today his influence lives on in a world wide movement, not only of Scouts and Guides and their senior and junior brothers and sisters, but in the B.-P. and Trefoil Guilds. Here in the Houses of Parliament, where I am writing this, the B.-P. Guild has a membership of about 100, including members of all political parties and both Houses - Commons and Lords. To our generation Scouting carries its own memories - the clubroom, camps by sea and river, in meadow or glen - but above all, memories of comradeship, of happy and worthwhile activity. But for very many it means even more than this - it means a code of conduct for the individual, in its application to national and international relations, pointing the way to happier Nations and a better world. Some of us may not be around for the bi-centenary - who can tell? - but one thing is certain, if the movement keeps B.-P.'s ideas and ideals ever before it, it will be stronger even than it is now, and it will have made a great contribution to the happiness of mankind.

Jubilee Journal, 8th August 1957

B.-P. at a Rally in 1923

THE HANDBOOK
SCOUTING FOR BOYS

The handbook that has been described as 'the match which lit the camp fires of the world', had as its full title: *Scouting for Boys, a Handbook for Instruction and Good Citizenship*. It had sketches, yarns, stories, advice and anecdotes for boys, and also separate advice for instructors/adults. It became a best seller, reputedly the third best selling book of all time (depending on which source one refers to).

B.-P. wrote a report of his Brownsea Island Camp in the autumn of 1907, and began a series of lectures to youth leaders and boys around the country. His handbook *Scouting for Boys* was initially published in fortnightly parts, starting *15th January 1908, priced 4d. Although it was a serial that many boys (adults too) began to collect and read with awe and excitement, initially it did not receive great reviews in the local and national press. Despite the many inspiring anecdotes and sketches from B.-P's own hand (with ideas lifted from many other sources too), its layout and content appeared quirky to many adults. For example, instructors were told to get boys used to the sight of blood by acquiring sheep's blood for first-aid practice. On the other hand, some of B.-P.'s advice of 1907 still seems wise today: *'There is no need to take all the drugs, pills, and medicines which you see so temptingly advertised; they often do you harm in the end.'*

Other ideas in the book show B.-P.'s wide reading and influences (for example, the decline of empires). His sketches and ideas on interpreting the physical characteristics of others, similarly, with its related topics of phrenology and social class or racial stereotyping, in addition to Darwinian theory may well have been connected with B.-P.'s family connection with Sir Henry Flower. The eminent zoologist and museum curator married B.-P.'s mother's sister in 1858. William Flower gave lectures on the Comparative Anatomy of Man, Human Crania, and similar topics. He stated that contact with Europeans must inevitably lead, sooner or later, to the disappearance of the inferior, or 'non-adaptive' races of mankind.

It had been a somewhat rushed affair and was produced on cheap paper (to help make it affordable to most boys). Although generally respectful and optimistic, some reviewers couldn't see how working-class boys from the towns and cities were going to be attracted to what they perceived to be B.-P.'s 'a life on the prairie' approach. Wearing shorts, walking around with broomsticks, doing things for others? It'll never take off!

---

*15th January has always been quoted in official sources though Percy Everett states that it was, in fact, published on the 16th January. He may well be correct: Everett visited B.-P. at Wimbledon whilst he was writing it (watching fascinated whilst B.-P., surrounded by a mass of papers, notes and sketches, added bits here and there, working freely with either hand) and, as Pearson's senior literary editor, oversaw the book's publication. In Everett's own book, *The First Ten Years,* he states: *'The first part was actually published on January 16th, 1908, the second on January 30th and the remaining four parts at fortnightly intervals...'*

John Hassall designed the front covers. One-time Vice-President of the London Sketch Club, he pioneered poster design. His railway poster 'Skegness is so bracing' holds the record for longevity and ubiquity (though he had not visited Skegness at the time of doing the poster!). He was later made a Freeman of Skegness, which entitled him to free entry to cinemas and free use of the deck-chairs.

The printing and publishing of Baden-Powell's *Scouting for Boys* very nearly came to a grinding halt. The print-works proprietor, Horace Cox, refused to allow B.-P.'s explicit writing on 'self abuse' to be included in the main body of the book, considering it to be obscene. It was eventually included in a re-edited version elsewhere in the book.

B.-P. ploughed all profits from the book into organising and developing his Boy Scouts scheme (which initially included paying the salaries of the small nucleus of Headquarters staff working from a tiny London office).

By 1909 it had been translated into five languages. Jeal also notes:

Twenty years after its first publication in Great Britain, the book was in print in 26 countries (not including all those within the British Empire) in roughly twice that many editions.... Scouting for Boys has probably sold more copies than any other title during the twentieth century with the exception of the Bible.

Since the very first published copy there have always been changes and additions (continuing after B.-P.'s death); also various editions: Memorial, Boys', and Definitive editions. Keen Scouts might have thought two errors in the Boys' edition, when it was first published, were deliberate tests of knowledge and skill! Two Morse code symbols remained incorrect until reprints were done.

Both Welsh and Braille editions have also been published.

More than 50,000 copies were sold in Britain forty years later, in 1948, the fortieth anniversary of its first publication. (Leaders were recommended to read it annually.)

In 1963 a 'definitive' edition included many previously unseen sketches by B.-P.

April 1999 saw the 5th printing of the 35th edition of *Scouting for Boys*. It was last published in 2004 (by OUP) with additional notes by Elleke Boehmer. Although it has not been officially used as a handbook for around four decades, sales continue year by year.

It was the original publication of the book in January 1908, in fact, that really launched the movement (to all intents and purposes the Scout movement really began in 1908 rather than 1907).

The *Daily Graphic* of January 1908 commented on the new book and organisation: *'That is a kind of 'snowball' organisation to which nobody could object'.*

Featured below is an extract from a review that appeared in *The Spectator.*

The first part gives an accurate enough notion of what General Baden-Powell hopes to achieve, and how. It is very unconventional, and whether the boyish fancy will be captured by the precise mixture of seriousness and madness which it prescribes as a working rule of life we cannot undertake to say. But let us hope that it will.

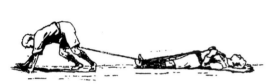

Dragging insensible man: both heads down near the floor

The boy who apes the man by smoking will never be much good

A strong and healthy boy has the ball at his feet

Ian Hislop, on BBC television and in the *Observer*, gave *Scouting for Boys* a good review in 2007, calling it 'bizarre, quite bonkers but also quite brilliant.'

THE SCOUT MOVEMENT: DID YOU KNOW?

The term 'Boy Scout' was in use long before Baden-Powell started his scheme. Popular in boys' comics, the first known use of 'Boy Scout' is believed to be in a series published by the Aldine Press in 1899. Entitled *The New Buffalo Bill Library,* it contained the following: *'The boy scout', one of Buffalo Bill's most trusted Scouts ... Harry White, a youngster of seventeen.* Additionally, the *Boys of the Empire* comic ran a serial in 1900 called *'The Boy Scout'.* It used B.-P.'s name and was based on his small army book *Aids to Scouting.*

Research by Robert Campbell records that the words BOY SCOUT were used by the firm Mackenzie & Mackenzie Ltd for their biscuits and cakes, they having gained protection on 12th December 1908 under class 42 of the Trademarks register.

Three quotes dubiously claiming new origins for the Scout movement:

King Arthur was the founder of British Scouts, Michael Rosenthal in 1986; he went on to say: *If eugenics is ever to be achieved in Great Britain it will come through the Boy Scouts and the Girl Guides.*

Hugh Brogan wrote in 1987: *If so, he can* [Rudyard Kipling] *claim to be one of the originators of the Boy Scout Movement.*

Lastly, in his biography of C. B. Fry, Iain Wilton wrote about the naturalist Ernest Seton's approach to Fry regarding interesting the famous athlete in starting a boys' woodcraft scheme. Wilton's inaccurate and oversimplified comment reads: *The answer, he concluded, was 'No' - a misjudgement which prevented him (rather than Baden-Powell) from becoming the founding father of British scouting. Nevertheless, C.B. still played a leading, and previously neglected, role in the scout movement.*

One of the last (if not the last) films Walt Disney saw through to completion was *Follow Me Boys!* Starring Fred MacMurray, it was about a jazz musician who becomes a Scoutmaster and starts up a Boy Scout Troop. Disney died in December 1966, the film was released in the UK in mid-1967.

The aim, principles and method of the Scout Association is to:

contribute to the development of young people in achieving their full physical, intellectual, social and spiritual potentials, as individuals, as responsible citizens and as members of their local, national and international communities.

Total numbers (all sections, adults and children) in the UK Scout movement in 2007: 818,963.

There are over 28 million Scouts world-wide.

In world-wide Scouting, the movement is growing. In former Communist countries Scouting is enjoying a revival. America and Asia have the highest Scout memberships in the world (in 2006):

Indonesia ~ 8,103, 835

United States ~ 5, 970, 203

Philippines ~ 1, 872, 525

The most recent members of the World Scout Organisation are: Albania, Guinea and Malawi.

Leaders in the movement are unpaid; all Scout Groups have to be self-financing.

William Stone, one of Britain's oldest males, can also perhaps be called Britain's oldest Scout. Reaching the age of 106 in 2007, William is thought to be the only surviving British veteran to have fought in both World Wars. As a boy he was a Scout in Kingsbridge, Devon. He recalled one of his first camps in about 1912 when they camped at East Portlemouth. On the return trip home by paddleboat ferry the boys were all singing "I don't care if the ship goes down - she don't belong to me!", which he was worried about.

The Scout Association in the 1970s was one of the biggest landowners in the country.

Many ordinary and famous people found their niche, inner strength, leadership potential or new interest through the Scouts. Although a few were lost to the Scouts after a very brief association, they were not necessarily all 'Scout failures': some found that through, for example, doing judo or swimming in the Scouts, they found a calling and wanted to pursue the activity in a more comprehensive way by joining specialist clubs. Unsurprisingly, one of the ornithologist Sir Peter Scott's first Scout badges was the Naturalist badge; astronaut Neil Armstrong had his interest in the Moon and Space awakened by doing the Astronomer badge.

In 1990 Scout Groups were given the option to accept girls as members if they wished.

Interestingly, today females may join any section of the Scouts as children or as adult warranted leaders; males may not join a Girl Guide section or become warranted leaders (though adult males can be helpers).

In one series of Channel Four's reality show Big Brother, the live-in contestants were challenged to pass the requirements of investiture for a Cub Scout. The contestants, having learnt the Law and Promise, were given uniforms and invested as 'honorary Cub Scouts'.

The Scout movement has continued to do many big good-turns. In the First World War it bought recreation huts for soldiers, and Scout ambulances. Included in its many later appeals was a new, fully equipped lifeboat (named *Scout*) purchased for the RNLI in 1975.

Boy Scouts have never had to rub two sticks together to pass a test.

Woggles are called woggles and not toggles. For nearly the first two decades of the movement's history there was no such thing as a woggle. The scarf was simply knotted at the top; a second knot was tied in the end of the scarf to remind the Boy Scout to do his daily good-turn.

According to the General Manager of the Scout Shop, in 1961 the three most popular Scout proficiency badges were (most popular first): Swimmer, First Aid, Firefighter. Three least popular: Rope Spinner, Piper, and Signaller.

In 2005 husband and wife Paul and Thea Bristow won £15 million on the lottery. As leaders in the 1st Torbay Scout Group, they paid for their Cubs, Scouts and leaders to travel on a privately chartered airliner and go on a two week adventure camp in Canada.

The Girl Guide movement, although a sister movement which has had close links with the Scouts since its inception, is an entirely separate movement.

The current Lord Baden-Powell (3rd Baron of Gilwell) lives in Surrey and has an interest in breeding American Quarter horses. In 2007 Lord Baden-Powell (grandson of the founder) was aged seventy.

Since 1967 there have been seven Scout Laws. In 1908 B.-P. drew up nine but a tenth was added in 1911.

FAMOUS FORMER SCOUTS

There are hundreds of well known people who have been members of the Scout movement; and also the Girl Guide movement: H M The Queen, Betty Boothroyd, Cherie Blair, Angela Rippon, Virginia McKenna, Claire Short MP, Joan Plowright, Jenny Eclair, Helen Fielding, JK Rowling...

Denis Norden, once a Scout in Clapton/Stamford Hill, perhaps wasn't entirely sure if it would be alright on the night:

I have this vivid memory of being dragged out of bed one morning at 2am to have a look at 'The Plough'. It was very interesting but I was glad to get back to bed. I also vaguely remember that I lost the Troop's trek-cart, but please don't press me on the details as they never knew who did it!

David Bellamy, in his autobiography *Jolly Green Giant,* reveals that Scouting helped to occupy boys' time (and stomachs) when there were privations and little to do during the war:

Late in 1944 G and I joined the Scouts and enjoyed a few happy years trailing trek- carts and learning the skills of woodcraft and camping, despite the fact that we were members of the First Belmont Air Scouts. Our headquarters was in the old school in Belmont Village and we went camping either near Box Hill in Surrey or on Sid Marshall's farm ...

Basing Farm was full of land girls and prisoners of war and, as food rationing was still firmly in force, some of the Patrol Leaders who, in those wartime days ran the show, became dab hands at catching rabbits for the pot. I used to go along and let the little ones out of their snares, although, I must admit I'd tuck into rabbit stew with a will. One day, as we were doing the rounds of the field, we found a fox dead in one of the snares and took it along to the POWs working in the fields. We wanted to ask how to skin it, so that we could make very special woggles. No sooner had we produced our prize exhibit than its skin was off and the gutted carcass was in their cooking pot. Well they were hungry too, despite the Geneva Convention.

Alan Titchmarsh, in his autobiography *Trowel and Error,* rakes over some rather different memories, of which only a small taster is provided below.

I was not a natural Scout. It all seemed a bit artificial. I'd been perfectly happy as a Wolf Cub, but I was younger then, and you could wear a warm green woolly rather than a short-sleeved khaki shirt. When I was eleven Uncle Bert gave me a copy of 'Scouting for Boys' by Baden-Powell. It was full of handy hints on making fires (which from my back garden efforts I could do already) and following a map, but I knew the moors like the back of my hand, and it seemed pointless to keep stopping to check contour levels and trig points.

One thing about the book irritated me more than any other: it showed the correct way to walk. The 'healthy boy' (who was pictured as a handsome youth with a square chin and bulging muscles) walked properly, striding forward with his arms swinging, his head and shoulders back, his mouth fixed in a rictus grin, his eyes gazing directly ahead of him. The unhealthy boy (his arms hanging limply by his sides like the missing link in one of Darwin's evolution engravings) was a chinless wonder with buck teeth, a sullen expression and a stoop. He was walking badly, dawdling along looking at the ground. This was plainly daft. Anyone interested in natural history will always walk along looking at the ground- it's where the wildlife and the flowers are...

He goes on to talk about initiation ceremonies at camp, but perhaps it would be prudent to turn towards more positive memories from other well known people.

Like many other famous comedians and actors, Neil Morrissey, as a Cub, got his first ever stage performance in a Scout show. Glaswegian Billy Connolly, after a great time in the Wolf Cubs (run by a 'posh woman from up the road'), graduated to the Scouts. Depite his high hopes of being in the Cobra or Buffalo Patrols being dashed - he was placed in the Peewits - he enjoyed himself in the Scouts and found Scouting gave him a love of the outdoors. According to his biographer and wife, Pamela Stephenson, this is something that has never left him.

England footballer David Beckham is a former Scout. In his autobiography he wrote:

I was a Cub and later went on to be a Scout, both of which involved football, so I was happy doing that. Also, we'd go camping and it was great to go away with a group of friends. You learn quite a bit about yourself when you're away from your family.

Photo right: Prince Andrew of the 1st Buckingham Palace Cub Pack

Scouts: in addition to attracting those of a comedic bent, many others donned the uniform for short or long periods. All those listed below are former Scouts (sometimes Cubs only). The late Kenny Everett, alas, donned the Scout uniform for only the briefest of moments, as he explains in his book *The Custard Stops at Hatfield*:

Scouts have to wear this hairy, woolly pullover and I remember getting very excited about the new uniform until I put it on: trousers first, which were fairly hairy, and then the pullover which I couldn't bear for more than ten seconds. I ripped it off instantly, feeling as though my chest was on fire, and rushed to the Scoutmaster to ask if I could be a Scout even if I didn't wear the uniform. 'You must be joking mate,' he said. 'That's the whole meaning of the word. You all look the same and that's that - no uniform, no Scout.'

So I went to Dad and explained that I couldn't be a Scout because I had artistic, delicate skin. You can imagine how that went down! Him a tugboat captain an' all. He got very upset but there was nothing for it. My semaphore days were over.

Sport ~ Graham Hill, Sir Stirling Moss, Peter Oosterhuis, Brian and Nigel Clough, Sir Trevor Brooking, Michael Owen, Kirk Stephens, Sir Steve Redgrave...

Music ~ Mike Sammes, Lonnie Donigan, Sir Paul McCartney, Val Doonican, David Grant, George Michael...

Comedy ~ Ken Dodd, Ronnie Corbett, Les Dawson, Jim Davidson, Arthur Smith, Harry Hill, Mike Harding, Billy Connolly CBE, Matt Lucas...

Acting ~ Sir John Mills, Sir Norman Wisdom, John Bardon, Edward Woodward, Lionel Jeffries, Bernard Cribbins, Derek Nimmo, Sir Derek Jacobi, Martin Shaw, Lord Attenborough...

Politics ~ Harold Macmillan, Lord Soper, Lord Pitt, Tony Benn, Sir Harold Wilson, Sir Geoffrey Howe, Sir John Major, Neil Kinnock...

Others ~ Henry Williamson, Sir Richard Branson, Sir Tim Rice, Simon Mayo, Doug Scott, Ray Mears, Michael Buerk, Kenneth Baker, Sir Michael Parkinson, John Craven...

Overseas ~ Jason Donovan, James Stewart, Richard Gere, Jacques Chirac, Ex-King Constantine of Greece, Nelson Mandela, Steven Spielberg.

A youthful Richard Attenborough   123

AN A TO Z OF SCOUTING AND B.-P. FACTS!

A is for Akela, leader of the Cubs. Akela in Hindi means: alone (kela, on the other hand, means banana!). There must be more than one new Cub, surely, who thought they were saying "I'll kill her! We will do our best" when, during the opening ceremony of the Cub Pack meeting, they should have been saying "Akela, we will do our best!".

B is for Bob-a-Job, started in 1949 ... It was 'Bob-a-Job' who ran in the Grand National in 1964, though not in a winning position! ... It is also for **Barlow** (Ken). The 'Pathfinder' portrait by well known Scout artist Ernest Carlos has graced an interior wall of the *Coronation Street* character's home for decades.

C is for Communism. In the 1950s a member of the movement was asked to return his badges, including the coveted Queen's Scout badge because, like his father, he became a Communist. The first Boy Scout ever to be dismissed for political reasons?

D is for the Doyly Carte Opera Company, who were the first to film a Gilbert and Sullivan opera. *The Mikado* was premiered (in 'glorious technicolor') at the Leicester Square Theatre in 1939, in aid of the Boy Scouts' Appeal Fund.

E is for the Eeengonyama chorus, which all self-respecting Scoutmasters were supposed to teach their boys. With the response of 'Invooboo. Yah bo! Invooboo', it apparently meant: He is a lion! Yes! he is better than that; he is a hippopotamus!

F is for February, which was the month of B.-P. and his wife's birthday: both on the 22nd. Other famous people born on February 22nd include ~ racing car driver Niki Lauda, actors Kenneth Williams and Sir John Mills, and tennis champion Michael Chang (he was actually the second child, born in the second month at 2.00pm in 1972; his highest world ranking was 2).

G Gin gan gooli! This campfire song hit the pop charts in November 1989. There was no Scouting connection however, as it was by band *Scaffold*, who had had much better luck with *Lily the Pink*. But there is a slim Scouting connection after all, *Lily the Pink* remained at number one until 8th January 1969, this being the same day and month when B.-P. died. (Actually, poet Roger McGough, former *Scaffold* member, had been in the Scouts.) The 8th January also saw the birth of E.P. - Elvis Presley in 1935.

H is for hyrax, a pet (about the size of a rabbit) bought for 5 pence which B.-P. kept in Kenya and was devoted to. **H** is also for **H**iawatha, son of composer Samuel Coleridge Taylor. His son became a Scout in Wallington Surrey (see photo on page 127).

I is for India, where even the founder of Scouting forgot the words to the Scout Promise! At a rally in India, B.-P. was in the process of investing social reformer Annie Besant. It was she who prompted him when he momentarily forgot the words.

J is for Japs, B.-P.'s affectionate term for the Japanese. Laughably he has been accused of being a racist, yet he was in awe of the Japanese, Zulus and many other cultures. He inspired and was in turn inspired by the hundreds of different cultures seen at the numerous World Jamborees: all 'Jolly fine chaps,' as he would say.

K is for Kipling. For a time Rudyard Kipling and B.-P. lived close to each other: Kipling at Burwash, Sussex, and B.-P. almost round the corner at Ewhurst Place. Kipling's son, John, attended B.-P.'s Sea Scout camp at Bucklers Hard, Hants.

L is for the London Sketch Club where B.-P. was a member, as was Sir Arthur Conan Doyle. Other famous visitors to the club included Charlie Chaplin. B.-P. and Doyle were also members of the Crimes Club.

M is for Mein Kampf, of which B.-P. read and commented: *'A wonderful book, with good ideas on education, health, propaganda, organisation etc. - and ideals which Hitler does not practise himself.'*

N is for nude swimming. One tends to forget that in rivers and camp swimming pools (including Gilwell Park) Scouts often swam starkers in earlier decades.

O is for 'Outlander', the name of the alternative Scout Promise members, for many decades, have been allowed to make in place of the usual Christian Promise that uses the words 'duty to God'. Scouts merely have to have a religion to be a member, they do not necessarily have to be Christians.

P is for Peter, B.-P.'s son (the 2nd Lord Baden-Powell). Peter carried on the family tradition of eccentricity by being well known for arriving at the House of Lords clad in shorts and with a rucksack on his back.

Q is for the *Quest*, Antarctic explorer Ernest Shackleton's expedition ship, which two Boy Scouts boarded to accompany Shackleton on his last expedition ... Mary Quant's spring collection of 1971 had an outfit titled 'Scout's Honour', and incorporated a broad-brimmed hat and shorts.

R is for Gang Show founder Ralph Reader, of whom comedian Mike Harding said *'He should be shot!'* (not a fan of Gang Shows but he did enjoy the Scouts and going on camps!). Sir Tim **R**ice is also a former Scout (Anneka Rice, on the other hand, is a former Girl Guide).

S is for smoking. It is not commonly known (except within the family) that, for a time, B.-P. enjoyed a smoke! ... Changing the subject, splits in the Scout movement, as in other organisations occurred. As early as 1909 there was a breakaway Scout movement in England called the British Boy Scouts (the 1970s would see another, the 'BP Scouts').

T is for Tintin. The creator of this world famous children's book character was Herge (pen name of Georges Remi). Born in 1907, Herge was a keen Catholic Boy Scout in Belgium, and started his career as an illustrator by working on his school's Scout magazine.

U is for the USA. Of the 12 Apollo astronauts, 11 were former Boy Scouts. At the 7th National Jamboree of America in 1969, astronaut and former Eagle Scout Neil Armstrong sent a message from the Moon to the 35,000 Scouts. With scientific experiments taken to the Moon was a Scout badge. Armstrong was early inspired to go to the Moon after working for his Scout Astronomer badge (American: patch).

V is for van Raalte. It was Charles van Raalte who welcomed B.-P. on to his island to run his rather strange 'boy scout camp'. Other places, such as the Isle of Wight, had been considered: Scouting's history might well have had a different location with a claim to fame. Sir Francis **V**ane, a Carthusian and one-time London Scout Commissioner, would defect and lead a breakaway movement, the British Boy Scouts, in 1910.

W is for the World Cup of 1966. Behind the scenes, Boy Scouts were deployed at Wembley to race photographic and news items to press offices and collection points. Two years earlier, most people would have known that the weather forecaster on BBC television was in the Scouts - although in 'mufti', on screen he always wore a Scout badge.

X is for X1: B.-P. played in the first eleven football team for his school, Charterhouse. He was an entertaining and talented goalkeeper. The initials **X.B.S.**, on the other hand, formed the official wireless telegraphy code signal allotted to the Boy Scouts by the Post Office authorities in 1913.

Y is for yob, which B.-P. wanted to reverse and make into boy: ideally, a boy of use to his family and country ... The **YMCA** was an organisation which did much to help promote the Scout movement through providing premises and inviting B.-P. to lecture to boys on his 'Peace Scouting' ideas before he published the handbook.

Z is for Zeppelin. During the First World War some Scout Troops hastily insured their premises against the risk of Zeppelin damage. **Zululand** was where B.-P. saw fighting action. He was a great admirer of Zulu culture, his home at Pax Hill had Zulu spears on the wall.

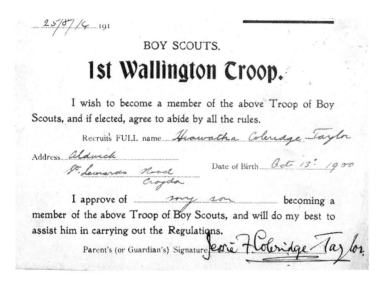

_25/8/14_ 191

BOY SCOUTS.

1st Wallington Troop.

I wish to become a member of the above Troop of Boy Scouts, and if elected, agree to abide by all the rules.

Recruit's FULL name _Hiawatha Coleridge Taylor_

Address _Aldwick_
St. Leonards Road
Croydon   Date of Birth _Oct 13. 1900_

I approve of _my son_ becoming a member of the above Troop of Boy Scouts, and will do my best to assist him in carrying out the Regulations.

Parent's (or Guardian's) Signature _S. Coleridge Taylor._

A COMPENDIUM OF SCOUT MOVEMENT
DATES AND EVENTS
(With Key Girl Guide Dates)

1857 Birth of Scouting's founder, Lord Baden-Powell, on the 22nd February.

1889 Birth of Olave Soames, future wife of Baden-Powell, and World Chief Guide (shares B.-P.'s birthday: 22nd February).

1900 The Siege of Mafeking ends on 17th May.

1907 B.-P.'s trial 'boy scout' camp held on Brownsea Island, Poole, Dorset, 29th July - 9th August. 20 boys in 4 Patrols, all trying out B.-P.'s boy scouting ideas.

1908 JAN 15 Part One of B.-P.'s handbook *Scouting for Boys* published; 4d each, issued fortnightly.

    APR 18 *The Scout* weekly paper for boys first published, price 1d.

    MAY 01 *Scouting for Boys* published as a complete book, 2/- (or 1/- for cheaper version).

    AUG/SEP First official (or 'proper') Scout camp held at Humshaugh, Northumbrian Moors with B.-P. Boys who collected the most coupons from *The Scout* paper attended (36 in all). It was also a very early chance for B.-P. to try out/impart some of his Scouting knowledge and ideas on leader training to the Scoutmasters who attended the camp.

1909 APR First Scouts to camp abroad. Patrol of eight taken by Headquarters' manager, Archibald Kyle, on a tour of Germany (included L. E. Sedgley of Walton-on-Thames and A. R. Dixon of Sutton). German 'boy scouts' (thought to be members of 'Vandervogel' organisation) toured England by train and foot that summer.

    MAY BBS (British Boy Scouts) breakaway Scout movement started in Battersea on Empire Day. Soon after led by Sir Francis Vane.

The National Boy Scout Headquarters (known as the BSA or Imperial Headquarters) had operated from Henrietta Street, a London office loaned by Pearson in 1908. In May 1909 they moved to independent premises at 116 - 118 Victoria Street, Westminster.

    JUL *Headquarters Gazette* magazine started, 3d monthly for Scoutmasters and Commissioners (later called *The Scouter*, this becoming *Scouting* magazine in 1971).

    JUL/AUG Large camp held on Salisbury Plain, and also another camp arranged for 200 boys at Wisley, Sussex.

    AUG (7th to 21st) B.-P.'s second (coupon) camp held for two weeks in Hampshire. One week as 'wet bobs' on C. B. Fry's training ship TS *Mercury*, moored on the river Hamble, then (rotating) one week as 'dry bobs' on land at Bucklers Hard. Attended by c100 boys, including Rudyard Kipling's son, John, also B.-P.'s nephew, Donald (who had also attended the Brownsea Island and Humshaugh camps).

SEP First national Scout Rally and Scoutmasters' Conference held at the Crystal Palace, south London. Attended by B.-P. and 11,000 Boy Scouts.

OCT The first Silver Wolf Badge was awarded to B. J. Fairfax Francklin, a Boy Scout in the 1st Syston Troop (originally awarded for gaining 24 proficiency badges, today it is presented to adult leaders in the movement with a record of outstanding service).

NOV The conditions for the King's Scout Badge were first published.
Boy Scouts took part in the Lord Mayor's Military Pageant (again in 1910 and later) - a Patrol of 8 Boy Scouts, each representing a Scout proficiency badge.
After Britain, Chile is the first known non-British Empire country to take up Scouting (during 1909).

DEC BSA Council and Executive was formed, with B.-P. as Chairman.

1910 Girl Guides officially formed. Agnes, B.-P.'s sister, first President.
B.-P. tours Canada with two Patrols of Scouts.

MAR 14 new proficiency badges introduced.

APR First national appeal for financial help made with the support of the *Daily Telegraph* newspaper.

SEP First annual census (UK): 100, 298 Boy Scouts; 7, 688 adult leaders.

OCT Sea Scout section officially launched (Sea Scout article in November's *HQ Gazette*).

1911 HQ publication of first rule book: *Boy Scout Regulations.*

JUN Boy Scouts on duty at Coronation of King George V.

JUL 26,000 Boy Scouts reviewed by the King at Windsor, the movement's second national rally. It included Scouts from Scotland and Canada. Devon Scouts, along with others, camped at Windsor. Many of the boys arrived in specially laid on trains: the first occasion some boys had ever travelled on one.

NOV Buckhurst Place Scout Farm, a large mansion with 96 acres in E. Sussex opened. Residential, run on Scout Patrol lines, it trained Scouts over the age of fifteen in all aspects of farming, with a view for some later emigrating (stifled by the war and dwindling new recruits, it closed in 1916).
First P.O.R. (Policy, Organisation and Rules) book published.

DEC A tenth Scout law was added to the original 9 (ten would remain until the major changes that followed publication of the *Advance Party Report* in 1966). 10th Law: 'A Scout is pure in thought, word and deed.'

1912 JAN Boy Scouts' Royal Charter of Incorporation. A few Troops even started to use 'Royal Scouts' on their headed paper!

APR London Commissioner appointed for Scouting in Special Schools.

AUG First major Scout disaster. Eight south London Boy Scouts drowned off Leysdown whilst sailing down the Thames to their summer camp site.

SEP The *Daily Mirror* presented a ketch named '*The Mirror*' to the movement. Extensive use made of it, but it sank in October 1913 following a collision in the Thames, with the loss of three Scouts and an Assistant Scoutmaster.

OCT B.-P. married Miss Olave Soames (30th October at St. Peter's Church, Parkstone). Some Scouts thought B.-P. had let them down! but they soon saw how Olave was prepared to work just as hard as her husband for the movement (and the Girl Guides).

NOV Sea Scouts took part in the Lord Mayor's Show.

1913 MAY Duke of Connaught appointed first President of the movement.

JUN Invitation received for a party of 50 Scouts to take part in a special camp in Denmark.

JUL 18,000 Boy Scouts at Birmingham Exhibition and Rally.

The Fenton Pearls, a comedy in three acts, was put on at the Savoy Theatre. Proceeds were for a fund to assist poor Troops.

SEP An Endowment fund was launched with a target of £250,000; the fund closed at £88,500 in December 1914.

1914 JAN Experimental scheme for Wolf Cubs (or 'Young Scouts') started for boys below the official minimum Scout age.

Similarly, Girl Guides started 'Rosebuds' (later called Brownies).

During Easter a Scoutmasters' Conference was held at Manchester Grammar School (organised by Scouting stalwart Roland Philipps). A Scout's Own (an act of non-denominational worship) was successfully attempted.

MAY First national Good-turn done to support Sir Arthur Pearson's work: Boy Scouts' Day of Work for the Blind. Also, Sir William Smith, founder of the Boys' Brigade, died.

JUN London Scouts were inspected on Horse Guards Parade by Queen Alexandra.

JUL It was announced in the *HQ Gazette* that a new rule had been passed by the Committee of the Council: *No Scout shall take part in any boat training till he can swim 50 yards.*

AUG Scouts enrol for War Service. Many deployed to despatch messages, watch the coast and guard reservoirs.

1915 SEP British Boy Scout Hut opened at Etaples, France, for the benefit of British Troops.

OCT 2nd Day of Work organised by B.-P. to raise funds for Scout Hut and Ambulance fund.

1916 FEB After numerous local Patrol Leader conferences, over 500 Patrol Leaders attended a conference in Manchester, with B.-P. present.

JUN First conference was held at HQ for all officers (as leaders were then called) interested in Cub work.

JUL Position of Senior Patrol Leader introduced.

SEP The Cornwell Badge instituted by B.-P. for boys showing great perseverance, bravery and devotion to duty. Former east London Boy Scout Jack Cornwell died from his wounds (June 1916) after serving on HMS *Chester* during the Battle of Jutland (he was posthumously awarded the Victoria Cross).

DEC The *Wolf Cub's Handbook* published.

Roland House Scout Hostel (29, Stepney Green) opened in east London. The Georgian house had been purchased by early Scouting pioneer, Roland Philipps. He fell in the Great War but had left the house to the movement. An extension (number 31 was purchased) opened in November 1936. Roland House eventually closed in December 1982.

Wolf Cub Display at Caxton Hall, London, to officially launch the new branch for boys aged nine to twelve. Many Cub Packs had already been formed by this time. *The Wolf Cub* was published monthly (December 1916 to 1920s, price 1d).

1917 MAR First Commissioners' Conference was held at Matlock Bath, Derbyshire. Later in the year a Commissioners' Conference was also held at Dunblane, Scotland.

MAY First (short-lived) scheme for Senior Scouts introduced.

JUN Moving from Victoria Street, June saw the opening of Imperial Headquarters at 25, Buckingham Palace Road, SWI. First official Scout Shop opened in the new Imperial HQ (though there had been an Equipment Department and numerous independent agents/shops for Scout uniforms).

1918 JAN Scout film *Be Prepared* premiered at the Great Assembly Hall, Mile End Road, east London. It was a movie but not a 'talkie'!

A Commissioners' Conference was held at the Albert Hall; B.-P. was present. This also included a Scout show/display, the first time the Albert Hall had been used by Scouts.

AUG The newly formed Senior Scout section renamed Rover Scouts.

1919 APR A national Scout memorial service was held in St. Paul's Cathedral.

JUL 26 New Scout campsite and training centre 'Gilwell Park', close to Epping Forest, opened. B.-P. and Olave present.

Northampton ship given to the Boy Scouts. Moored at Blackfriars.

SEP 8th - 19th First Wood Badge leader training course held at Gilwell (sculptor and artist Don Potter was one of the trainees; B.-P. visited).

1920 Girl Guides start Sea Guides for girls interested in water activities.

Youlbury Scout campsite, Oxford opened.

AUG First International Scout Conference and World Jamboree held at Olympia, London. Scouts were based/camped in Richmond Park (though were briefly flooded out and enjoyed local hospitality). Members of the public paid to see the daily displays of Scouting skills and entertainment. B.-P. acclaimed Chief Scout of the World. Under Mr. Hubert Martin of the Foreign Office, an international Scout council/bureau was established to promote the international Scout brotherhood.

1921 Death of William de Bois MacLaren, who bought Gilwell Park for the BSA; also death of Sir Arthur Pearson (in December), Scouting's publisher and sponsor.
    SEP First of the annual Gilwell Reunions.
Two Boy Scouts selected for explorer Shackleton's last Antarctic expedition.

The 1920s, for the first time, saw the use of woggles (rather than knotting the uniform scarf).

1922 JUN Publication of *Rovering To Success.*

    JUN 02 'Foxlease', Guides' Camping/Training Centre in the New Forest was opened. Also, Girl Guides granted Royal Charter of Incorporation.
    JUL Accredited representatives of Scout Associations met in Paris and established the International Scout Conference for the coordination of the Scout movement throughout the world.
    OCT 65,000 Boy Scouts and Wolf Cubs attended a 'Posse of Welcome' to the Prince of Wales, who was returning from a tour abroad. It was held at the Alexandra Palace, north London, and was attended by Rudyard Kipling, also Wolf Cub Peter, B.-P's son. (The Palace had been used since at least 1912 for local Scout displays and rallies. B.-P. himself attended a local one in 1913.)
World Scout membership exceeded 1 million.

1923 Kandersteg Scout Chalet, Switzerland, opened as *'a centre for camping and climbing to which all Scouts from all countries can go'* (soon coming under the auspice of the Scout Alpine Club). Originally a workers' chalet for men working on the Lotschberg railway tunnel (1906 - 1913), the old chalet was left abandoned after the tunnel was opened. It was more officially opened as an International Scout Centre in August 1926.
B.-P's preferred term 'Scouter', used as a general term for adult uniformed leaders in the movement, was not favoured by Lord Meath and other senior figures in the movement. By 1923, however (and to this day), it became a desired and commonly accepted term of reference (also in 1923 the monthly magazine titled *Headquarters Gazette* became *The Scouter*).

1924 AUG The 2nd World Jamboree was held in Ermelunden, Denmark.
Imperial Jamboree also held. 12,461 British and overseas Scouts camped at Wembley Paddocks (with catering by Messrs. Lyons; most went on to the World Jamboree afterwards).
Special tests for disabled Scouts were introduced (though disabled boys had been in the Scouts practically from the beginning). Later known as: the Extension branch; Handicapped branch (1936); today Scouts with 'special needs' are

integrated into local Scout Groups.

1925 DEC First Scout Music Festival held at the Royal College of Music.

1926 FEB Girl Guides make 22nd February (joint birthday of B.-P. and Olave) an annual occasion known as 'Thinking Day'.

APR First of many national Rover Moots ('get togethers', some being World Moots). This one was held over the Easter weekend at the Royal Albert Hall, London.

May General Strike. Surrey County Rally cancelled. Some Rovers became 'Specials' and assisted during the national crisis.

1927 JAN First of many Roland House Scout Centre pantomimes.
500 Scouters and Captain Robson, the Boys' Brigade leader who assisted B.-P. with his camp of 1907, revisited Brownsea Island as part of the Bournemouth Scout Conference.
'Polyapes' in Cobham, Surrey: land purchased as a memorial to Scouts of Kingston who lost their lives in the First World War. Later opened as a Scout campsite.

JUN Rosemary Home for Boy Scouts, Herne Bay opened with 22 boys in residence. It was a gift from Dr and Mrs. Colebrook, in memory of her brother Colonel Charles Campbell OBE, for Scouts recovering from illness. First warden: J.R. Stanley (it was more officially opened later in the year). It closed in 1939.

NOV The Chartered Association (Boy Scouts Association) Protection Order was issued, which gave legal protection for badges, names and connected titles.

1928 JAN Introduction of the Group system of registration. Wolf Cub Packs and Boy Scout Troops registered nationally at IHQ as being one combined unit.

JUL 21st Anniversary Reunion of the first Boy Scout Brownsea Island campers with B.-P. (some of whom lost their lives in the Great War).
World Association of Guides and Girl Scouts was set up.

1929 JAN Downe campsite, near Biggin Hill, Kent, acquired. Opened for general Scout camping in 1930 (run by IHQ in 1948). Ralph Reader's first London Gang Show was organised in 1932 to raise funds for a swimming pool at Downe.

JUN Frylands Wood, Addington, Surrey, acquired as a Scout campsite. Local Scout campsites all over Britain were acquired during the 1920s and 1930s.

JUL/AUG To celebrate the movement's coming of age, a world Jamboree was held at Arrowe Park, near Birkenhead. At a speech B.-P. told the large assembled gathering: *You are taking part in the biggest concourse of boys that has ever come together in the history of the world; not only that, but also it is a*

concourse of jolly fine boys, the best from every civilised country in the world.
50,000 Scouts took part (coming from Iraq, Ceylon and many other places). As
was traditional whenever B.-P. attended a rally or Jamboree, there was plenty of
rain and mud (hence its nickname of Mudboree). Being genuine campers, like
everyone else, B.-P. and the Prince of Wales slept in real tents. B.-P. set up a
'Development Committee' for the movement after the Coming-of Age Jamboree.

DEC The Deep Sea Scout branch was formed for Scouts/Leaders working
at sea and wanting to keep/get in touch with Scouts in ports world-wide.

1931 World Scout membership: 2,039,349. *Camping Standards* first published, a
certificated scheme to keep up standards in camping. The Road Traffic Act of
1931 affected the way Scouts could be transported to camp (in theory: many
Scouts still trundled along to camp sitting on their kit in the back of waggons
and lorries).
The first World Moot for Rover Scouts was held at Kandersteg Scout Chalet,
Switzerland (again in 1953 for the fifth Moot).

1932 OCT First London Scout Gang Show at the Scala Theatre; produced by
'anonymous Rover' Ralph Reader (three nights; was attended by B.-P. and
Olave).
Our Chalet, the first World Guide Centre, was opened in Switzerland.

1933 500 London Scouts spent a day at the GWR Railway Works, Swindon.
Also, Kingsdown, near Deal, Kent, was purchased by P. B. Nevill (a prominent
figure in Scouting) as a summer retreat. By 1936 he had built a bungalow on it.
After the Second World War, Scouts were invited to camp there. The Scout
Association took over the site during the 1970s (P. B. Nevill having bequeathed
it to them).

AUG Fourth World Jamboree held in the Royal Forest, Godollo, Hungary.

1934 FEB A Rover Scout Conference held in the Milton Hall, Manchester.

APR First National parade of King's Scouts held at Windsor Castle.

1935 APR First series of five Scout Training Courses held around the UK.

MAY King George V's Silver Jubilee. Many processions and celebrations.
3,750 London Scouts helped to sell programmes. In the evening Scouts across the
country, having built a chain of 1775 beacons, lit them (these had had to be
guarded against premature merriment from locals). The King lit the central one in
Hyde Park. Beacons were also lit in British territories overseas, with B.-P. doing
the honours in Winnipeg, Canada.

JUL World Rover Moot, Sweden.

AUG A special camp held for handicapped Scouts at Woodlarks, Farnham.

1935 - 39 First of the special Train Cruises for Scouts run by *The Scout* paper.
The train of sleeping and dining cars left Kings Cross and headed for Scotland.

Stopping at various places it returned to London at the end of one week (in 1937 Scouts paid £5.5s to attend the cruise).

1936 APR First production of Ralph Reader's show *Boy Scout* at the Royal Albert Hall.

AUG Great Tower campsite, close to Lake Windermere, officially opened by B.-P. It had been given to the BSA by William Wakefield, who had been an early Scout Inspector of B.-P.'s and attended his second camp at Humshaugh.

NOV An extension to Roland House Scout Hostel was opened. This extension, number 31, Stepney Green had been hampered by delays.

1937 APR Broadstone Warren campsite, Ashdown Forest, Sussex was opened to Scouts (on lease from the Manor Charitable Trust).

MAY Phasels Wood Scout campsite, Hertfordshire, opened.
Boy Scouts were on duty at Coronation of King George V1. In addition to selling programmes, Rover Scouts were used by the police to form a human barrier and help crowd control in Trafalgar Square. Most had started duties at four in the morning.

JUL Fifth World Jamboree, Holland. The last attended by B.-P.

OCT RRS *Discovery*, the ship used by explorer Scott of the Antarctic, was transferred to IHQ. It was moored on the Thames and used as a Sea Scout training ship.

NOV The Gang Show appeared in the Royal Command Performance at the London Palladium (the first amateurs to do so, this would occur in later years too). The film *Gang Show*, which used members of the cast and Ralph Reader, was shot at Pinewood Studios. It was premiered at the Lyceum Theatre.

1938 B.-P.'s name submitted to the Nobel Peace Prize Committee (for 1939) but no prize was awarded due to the outbreak of war.
Chalfont Heights Scout campsite, Buckinghamshire came into use.

NOV A Joint Committee set up by the London Scout Council and National HQ is appointed to explore the possibilities of obtaining more camping grounds around London.
The Boy Scout Fund was launched at Mansion House (£263,000 raised).

1939 JAN The first Gilbert and Sullivan opera to be filmed was *The Mikado*. It was premiered at the Leicester Square Theatre (in glorious technicolor) and was given in aid of the Boy Scouts' Appeal Fund.

JUN First Scout Soap Box Derby was staged at Brooklands Race Track, Surrey (the then editor of *The Scout*, Haydn Dimmock, had got the idea from the Boy Scouts of America). Resuming in 1950, it became known as the National Scoutcar Races.

JUL Third World Rover Moot held 15th - 26th July at Monzie Castle, Crieff, Scotland. 3,500 Rovers from 42 nations attended, including the countries (or representatives from): Poland, Hungary, South Africa, Norway, Nigeria, Iraq and Armenia. Prince Emanuel of Liechtenstein and Prince Gustaf Adolf of Sweden were among the campers.

NOV The Admiralty requested for Boy Scouts to volunteer for Convoy signaller duties. Many other war duties undertaken, for example: collecting salvage, erecting shelters, helping with evacuation and fitting gas masks.

1940 Roland House requisitioned by the War Office (bombed in September).

NOV Gilwell Park Scout Campsite/Training Centre requisitioned by the War Office.

1941 JAN 08 Death of Baden-Powell, Scouting's founder (in Kenya, aged 83).
B.-P. Memorial service held in Westminster Abbey (January 27th).
Air Scout branch officially launched. First national Air Scout camp held for P.L.s/Seconds at Avington Park, Hants.
Lord Somers, KCMG, DSO, MC, elected Chief Scout of the British Empire.

APR The new Chief Scout, Lord Somers, appointed a commission to *'make recommendations to the Committee of the Council as to the post-war development of the Scout Movement'*. Its report, *'The Road Ahead'*, was published in 1945.

SEP Bradley Wood Scout campsite, Yorkshire, was acquired.

1942 APR B.-P. Memorial Fund was launched on St. George's day.

DEC National Air Scout Exhibition, in London's West End. Rex Hazlewood, Travelling Commissioner, organised a large-scale Air Scout Exhibition at Dorland Hall. Some 10,000 visitors came during its 6 days of opening; a distinguished air hero performed the opening ceremony each day.
First All England Air Scout Camp held in Avington Park, Hants.
The Duke of Gloucester was appointed President of the BSA.

1943 MAY Senior Scout scheme was published for comment in *The Scouter*.

JUL Gilwell Camp Chief J. S. Wilson resigned, John Thurman appointed.

1944 MAR First party from Boy Scouts' International Relief Service Workers go to Greece (the Service was designed to help civilians and Scouts in need).

MAY Scouts' Day of Work raised £33,000 for Scouts' International Relief Service.

1945 APR Lord Rowallan, KT, KBE, MC, TD, LLD, DL, elected Chief Scout of the British Commonwealth and Empire.
Girl Guides' Air Rangers section was officially launched.

1946 MAR Preliminary Training (prior to taking Wood Badge training) was introduced. The Gilwell (two strand leather Turk's head) woggle was introduced.

APR The first Medals for Meritorious Conduct were awarded

AUG An organisation for British Scouts in Germany was established.

OCT The Senior Scout section was officially started (and new plan for Rover Scouts); also, a revised scheme for proficiency badges came into force.

1947 APR A Scout and Guide Memorial stone to B.-P. was unveiled on St. George's Day, in Westminster Abbey by the Duke of Gloucester.

JUL Approximately one third of the original manuscript of *Scouting for Boys* was discovered and given to the BSA. King George V1 reviewed Commonwealth Scouts at Buckingham Palace.
First Handicapped Scout Camp held at Downe, Kent. Such camps later acquired the name 'Agoonoree', taken from the Dutch Scout Association's first international 'Agoonoree' camp for handicapped Scouts in 1949 (Greek derivation of 'Agoon' meaning: a meeting, a competition or collection).
At an International Conference, a resolution was passed recommending that all National Scout Associations should proceed with the formation of Old Scouts Associations in time for the 40th birthday of Scouting.

AUG 6th World Jamboree (Jamboree of Peace) held in Moisson, France.

1948 APR Organisation of staff at Headquarters leads to the full-time position of a Chief Executive Commissioner, with A.W. Hurll being the first appointed CEC.

JUN B.-P. Guild of Old Scouts inaugurated at the Royal Albert Hall (became 'Scout Fellowship' in March 1976). The Salvation Army became recognised as a sponsoring authority for running Scout Groups. Also in June, Sir Percy Everett, publisher Sir Arthur Pearson's literary editor, who had visited B.-P. whilst he stayed at a friend's house on Wimbledon Common and wrote parts of *Scouting for Boys*, returned to unveil a plaque. Attached to the windmill, the plaque commemorated B.-P.'s stay in the house next to the windmill, where he wrote parts of the famous handbook. Everett's visit (he was by then Deputy Chief Scout) was part of a large Scout show/display held on the Common and run by local Scout Districts.

JUL The first rally for university Scout and Guide Clubs and Rover Scout Crews was run at Youlbury Scout campsite, near Oxford.

OCT First National Conference, Filey. Also, Scouts assisted at the Olympics held in England.

DEC Brynbach Scout campsite, Wales, was transferred to the BSA (it was closed in September 1952).

1949 What has become the well known annual Devizes to Westminster Canoe Race started in 1949 as a challenge by local businessmen. Local Rover Scouts were challenged to paddle to London in under 100 hours, they managed it in 89 hrs 50 mins.

APR Originally the idea of Haydn Dimmock, the editor of *The Scout,* the first 'Bob-a-Job Week' was launched. £23,600 was received into the movement's central funds. By 1955 it brought in £45,000 annually to help run the movement. In 1970, anticipating decimalisation the following year, it became known as

Scout Job Week (by the 1990s few Scout Groups used the Bob-a-Job scheme).

MAY The beret became optional alternative headwear for Senior Scouts, Rover Scouts and Scouters.

AUG First international camp for handicapped Scouts held in Holland.

Also, the fourth World Rover Moot was held in Norway.

1950 AUG Loss of the 1st Mortlake's whaler *Wangle 111* and entire crew of ten Sea Scouts in the English Channel.

SEP The Scout Soapbox Derby resumed (last held in 1939).

OCT Introduction of the RAF recognition scheme for Air Scout Troops.

NOV Following much debate, hitch-hiking was forbidden for Scouts except in emergencies.

DEC First London Gang Show was held since the war.

1951 Queen Elizabeth 11 became Patron of the Scout Association in succession to her late father.

AUG The 7th World Jamboree was held in Bad Ischl, Austria.

1952 JAN - APR Chief Scout Lord Rowallan toured the Caribbean (with many other tours over the following years).

FEB Sir Percy Everett, former Deputy Chief Scout, died the day after B.-P.'s birthday. Also, Perry Wood Scout campsite, Surrey, acquired by the BSA.

APR An extra 'bob' (shilling/5p) was added to the annual Bob-a-Job to go towards National HQ's finances (before HQ introduced an annual members' fee).

JUL First World Indaba (for Scouters) took place at Gilwell Park.

1953 JUN Boy Scouts were on duty at the Coronation of HM Queen Elizabeth 11 (when making the Promise, Scouts and leaders were reminded of their duty to God and the Queen, not, as it had been since 1908, the King!). Gilwell was given the Honorary Freedom of the Borough of Chingford.

The World Rover Moot was held at Kandersteg, Switzerland.

1954 MAR A debate in the House of Lords followed the motion from Viscount Stansgate that '...*in the opinion of this House the imposition of political and religious tests by the Boy Scout Movement is foreign to its Charter and purpose and repugnant to our national tradition and liberty of conscience.*' The Motion was well defended by Lord Rowallan, and no speakers supported Lord Stansgate.

SEP The beret became permitted alternative uniform headwear for all Boy Scouts (already worn by Air Scouts).

OCT A special committee was formed to consider a report on the declining numbers of Scouts.

1955 APR Grants totalling £50,000 were awarded to the movement from the King George V1 Foundation.

JUL Scott's RRS *Discovery*, its upkeep burdensome, was returned to the

Admiralty.

The first Scout Gliding course was held at Lasham, Hants. Also, at the BSA's AGM a new scheme was approved which saw a reconstituted and more representative governing body of the Association.

8th World Jamboree: 1000 British Scouts attended the World Jamboree at Niagara-on-the-Lake, Canada at a subsidised cost of £160.00 each.

First Cub Day held at Gilwell Park. Attendance was said to be 7,800; by 1968 it was over 29,000 (with sponsorship from Schweppes).

1956 FEB International Scout Club was formed.

MAR The first wide-spread Patrol Leader training courses were introduced.

APR *'Rover Plan'* : new rules for Rover Scouts published.

JUN *Scouts of Tomorrow* report on declining numbers was published. Also, 1,800 Cubmasters camped for a week at Gilwell Park.

SEP First Commissioners' Conference for twenty years, held in Skegness.

1957 JAN Lord Somers House, a home for 14 working men opened in Ilford, Essex. It served as a local Scout headquarters, and the residents supported local Scouting in their spare time.

FEB Centenary of the birth of B.-P. Service held at Westminster Abbey.

B.-P. Memorial Fund public appeal launched at Mansion House.

MAR Lord Rowallan was granted the Freedom of the City of Edinburgh.

MAY Troop Leaders' and Patrol Leaders' National Camp held at Gilwell.

JUN National Collective Good Turn Week. Longridge Scouting Boating Centre, Marlow, Bucks, was opened by Sir Cecil Harcourt.

JUL Chief Scout Lord Rowallan unveiled a locomotive named in his honour. Also, Lord Maclay, the President of the Boys' Brigade, and the Earl of Scarborough were appointed Vice-Presidents of the BSA.

AUG World Golden Jubilee Jamboree, Indaba & Moot (titled 'JIM') held at Sutton Coldfield, near Birmingham. With 35,000 participants, it was the 9th World Jamboree and commemorated the centenary of B.-P.'s birth and fifty years of Scouting. It was opened by the Duke of Gloucester, who arrived by helicopter. It was also visited by the Queen and Prime Minister. The GPO issued commemorative stamps. Radio Luxembourg gave free 'air time' during the week preceding the Jamboree for 'The Voice of Scouting'. One former Scout recalled in centenary year being delighted in fooling hundreds of Jamboree Scouts by dressing in silk pyjamas and claiming to be the Sultan of Malacca.

NOV The Gang Show again in Royal Variety Performance (also in 1964).

DEC A special committee was appointed to review Scouter training.

1958 APR A European 'Duty to God' conference was held at Gilwell.

JUL The Third International Camp for Handicapped Scouts was held at Gilwell Park; visited by Princess Alexandra.

AUG An obelisk, in commemoration of the 1957 World Jamboree, was unveiled at Sutton Park, Sutton Coldfield.

OCT First Jamboree-on-the-Air (JOTA, for Ham radio enthusiasts).

NOV Sir Harold Gillett, a former Scout District Commissioner who went on to hold high and influential positions within the movement, became Lord Mayor of London.

1959 JUN *Boy Scout* by Ralph Reader put on at the Royal Albert Hall.

JUL 10th World Jamboree, Mount Makiling, Philippines. The first World Jamboree in the Far East, attended by 12,203 Scouts from 44 countries.
Gremtu, a Gremlin sailing-dinghy designed by Percy Blandford, was built by Newbold-on-Stour Sea Scouts and displayed at the National Boat Show.

SEP Sir Charles Maclean, KT, GCVO, KBE, was appointed Chief Scout of the Commonwealth.

1960 AUG National Sea Scouts' Jubilee Camp. Also, the third World Scouters Indaba was held in the Netherlands.

Coca-Cola the 'healthy drink' sponsored the first National Scout Camp-Cooking competition, held at Gilwell Park.

SEP 34th Gilwell Reunion held. The Reunion was open only to members of the '1st Gilwell Park Scout Group' (all those who held the Wood Badge; holders paid an annual subscription).

1961 JUN Scottish Rover Moot held at St. Columbia's Isle; over 400 attended.

JUL Baden-Powell House Scout Hostel, South Kensington, London, opened by the Queen. Bed and breakfast for boys (dormitory): 10s. 6d; £3.3s. per week. Also, the movement's first ('official') history published: *B.-P.'s Scouts*, by Collis, Hurll and Hazlewood.

SEP The 2nd Commonwealth Scout Conference took place at Baden-Powell House (the first had been held in New Delhi, India in 1959).

NOV Senior and Rover Scouts were given the option of wearing long uniform trousers (colours lovat or dark blue). These could be purchased at £2.10s a pair.
The Scouter of November - December issue highlighted facts about the BSA 1961 census, revealing that: 43 % of English Scout Groups were 'open' Groups; 57 % were sponsored; 46.7 % of all Groups were in churches; 7.3 % were in schools.

DEC The seventh World Rover Moot was held in Australia.

1962 JUN The Air Scout branch came of age.
The National Trust purchased Brownsea Island (the Scout and Guide Associations contributed funds also; they were given special camping rights).
World Scout membership reached 9.3 million (UK: 581,512 members).

AUG First exchange visit of Scouts with the USA.

SEP The 2nd Boy Scouts' European Conference was held in Hove, Sussex.

1963 MAY Brownsea Island was officially opened to the public.

AUG The 11th World Jamboree was held in Marathon, Greece.

1964 JAN First meeting of the Chief Scout's Advance Party (to assess and review the state of the movement and plan comprehensively for its future).

Introduction of an annual capitation fee (5/-) by IHQ for all members.

FEB BBC Television broadcasted a special *Songs of Praise* programme from Baden-Powell House, 400 Guides and Scouts present.

APR In Ilford, Lord Somers House, named after the Chief Scout, closed. It had started in Brandon Street, Southwark in 1946. Being the property of S. J. Marsh, the Scoutmaster who was involved in the Leysdown Sea Scout tragedy of 1912, he'd left his Brandon Street house to South London Scouts. With the lease nearing its end, it was closed in 1953. A new Lord Somers House was opened in Ilford, east London in 1957.

OCT First official visit of British Boy Scouts to Japan.

1965 MAY The first National Scout Band Championships were held in Bramcote, Warwickshire. Supreme Champions: 13th Coventry; Runners-up: 1st Newport. Also in May: first National Father and Son Camp at Gilwell Park; 1,250 attended.

1966 JAN Golden Jubilee year for Wolf Cubs.

FEB The Scout and Guide Founder's Day Service was part of Westminster Abbey's 900th Anniversary Celebrations.

JUN Publication of the Chief Scout's *Advance Party Report*. Sweeping changes followed in policy, uniform, terminology and programme. Terms such as **Wolf** (as in Wolf Cub) and **Boy** (Boy Scout) were dropped, along with the uniform colour khaki, the big hat, pole (stave) and shorts (except for Cubs).

SEP *The Scout* weekly paper ceased publication.

OCT A revised wording of the Scout Law and Promise was introduced.

NOV The Girl Guide Association published their own major review of programme and training.

DEC Special BBC Television *Songs of Praise* programme was recorded at the Metropolitan Tabernacle, Elephant and Castle, to celebrate the 50th anniversary of Cub Scouts.

1967 The Greater London Festival of Music and Drama was held for Scouts.

MAY The Boy Scouts Association renamed The Scout Association.

JUN 'Scout Week' held to celebrate the movement's Diamond Jubilee (various displays and Groups showing films/holding open nights).
SSAGO (the Student Scout and Guide Organization) was formed for Scouts and Guides at university or college. Also, the BP Guild was set up for members over 20 who did not necessarily want to hold a leader's warrant but wanted to support Scouting.
Lastly, in June, the move of the Equipment Department/Scout Shops to Churchill

Industrial Estate, Lancing (on the site of Lancing Railway Carriage Works) took place; previously a warehouse in Clapham had been used to service Scout Shop branches.

AUG 12th World Jamboree held in Farragut State Park, Idaho, USA. In England a National Patrol Leaders' Camp was held on Brownsea Island; a memorial stone was unveiled close to the site where B.-P.'s experimental camp had taken place in August 1907. It was unveiled by the Hon. Mrs. Betty Clay CBE.

OCT Following the recommendations of the Chief Scout's *Advance Party Report*, the implementation of a new training scheme and phasing in of new uniforms was started (Rover Scout and Senior Scouts sections were replaced with Venture Scouts).

1968 JAN Prince Andrew joined the Cubs (HM The Queen an ex-Girl Guide).

MAR Three National Scout Activity Centres announced: Lasham, Hants (Air), Longridge, Bucks (Water), and Whernside, Yorks (Caving).
First Gilwell Fleur-de-Lys Ball (fundraiser) held.

APR Prince Philip, accompanied by Prince Andrew, took the salute at the annual Windsor parade.

MAY The first National Scout and Guide 'Folk Fest' was held at B.-P. House (there had been Scout Folk Festivals in 1966/7 in Amersham). The National event of 1968 was sponsored by *The Scouter* and sold out quickly. A second Folk Fest was held in November of the same year (others followed).
First National Scout Family Camp held at Gilwell Park.

JUN The first National Scout and Venture Scout Kart Championships were held at Buckmore Park, Chatham. Also, the first National Scout Cyclo-Cross meeting, sponsored by Elswick-Hopper Cycles. World Scout membership: 11,981,737.

1969 FEB First Scout and Guide Philatelic Exhibition at Baden-Powell House.

APR The 1st Scottish Scout and Guide Folk Fest was held at B.-P. House, Edinburgh.
Introduction of 'Minimum Standards' to be applied to all Groups.

MAY Mixed Ranger/Venture Scout Units permitted (later 'Joint Units').

JUN National Pack Scouters' Camp held at Gilwell Park.

JUL To benefit the Scout Association, a Royal Gala performance of the film *Alfred the Great* took place at The Empire Theatre, Leicester Square.

AUG Scout Holiday Homes Trust, founded by Charles Porter, was adopted by the BP Scout Guild and inaugurated as a registered charity (absorbed by The Scout Association in 1970). The Archers' Walter Gabriel (Chris Gittens) was National Vice-President of the BP Scout Guild and a keen supporter. Open to members of the Scout and Guide movements, and also non-members, the Trust (2005) had 15 caravans, 2 chalets in 13 sites nationwide for those with special needs, families on low income and/or facing other difficulties.

SEP National Scout Leaders' Camp, Gilwell Park.

1970 JAN A Scout and Guide marina was displayed at the International Boat Show.

FEB 3rd Folk Fest held at the Fairfield Hall, Croydon.

MAR Anticipating decimalization in 1971, Bob-a-Job became 'Scout Job Week'.

APR Queen's Guides, celebrating the Girl Guide movement's Diamond Jubilee, joined the Scout movement's annual parade of Queen's Scouts at Windsor.

SEP A National Patrol Leaders' Council was organised in 5 camps across Britain.

The 'BP Scouts', a small breakaway Scout movement, was formed; it encouraged Scout Groups to return to pre-*Advance Party Report* days, with more traditional Scout training and use of the original Scout uniform and badges.

OCT 2nd annual camp for Scout radio/electronic enthusiasts held at Phasels Wood campsite, Herts.

The National Scout Lawn Tennis Championships were also held during 1970.

1971 JAN A new purple World Membership badge was introduced for British Scouts. *The Scouter* magazine, formerly the *HQ Gazette*, was renamed *Scouting* (price 10p).

FEB World Chief Guide, Olave Lady Baden-Powell, attended the London premiere of Scout film *These are Scouts*.

AUG 480 British Scouts attended the 13th World Jamboree held at Asagiri Heights, in the foothills of Mount Fuji, Japan.

DEC Folk Fest 5 was held at the Royal Albert Hall.

1972 APR The Duke of Kent reviewed 500 Venture Scouts who had gained the Queen's Scout Award, in a new style ceremony at Windsor Castle.

JUL Sir William Gladstone Bt, DL, MA, was appointed the new Chief Scout of the UK and overseas branches.

OCT The Queen and the Duke of Edinburgh attended the 40th Anniversary year of Ralph Reader's Gang Show (the final one was in 1974).

World Scout membership: 13,110,259.

1973 SEP More than 30 European Scout Public Relations Officers attended a conference on Scouting's public relations, at Baden-Powell House.

1974 AUG The Committee of the Council (the Scout Association's ruling body) appointed a Working Group to consider how to maintain and improve adult support for Scouting's 600,000 members in the UK.

OCT Ralph Reader presented his last London Gang Show (held at the Gaumont State Theatre, Kilburn).

DEC The Buckingham Palace Road Scout Association Headquarters remained only as the Scout Shop; the Scout Association departments moved to Baden-Powell House, Gilwell Park and Lancing whilst awaiting completion of a new extension to Baden-Powell House (completed in July 1976).

1975 JAN The Scout Association launched a new corporate identity symbol - 'Scouts' - incorporating the fleur-de-lys badge in place of the letter 'o' in Scouts.

FEB The Duke of Kent was appointed President of the Scout Association.

APR The annual Capitation (members') Fee was £1.00.

JUL The 14th World Jamboree at Lillehammer, Norway, was opened by the King of Norway. 17,700 Scouts from 93 countries attended; the UK contingent was led by Lord Robert Baden-Powell, grandson of the founder.

1976 JAN Cub Scouts' Diamond Jubilee commenced.

JUL Olave Lady Baden-Powell visited the new Scout Association headquarters at Baden-Powell House.

SEP Girls were permitted to join Venture Scout Units. Also, the B.-P. Scout Guild (later called Scout Fellowship) held its National Conference at Nottingham University.
The first Scout and Guide National Symphony Orchestra course took place.

NOV The Queen opened the new Headquarters at Baden-Powell House.

DEC A Scout and Guide joint Jubilee badge went on sale to support the Queen's Silver Jubilee Appeal.

1977 JUN 25 Olave, Lady Baden-Powell, wife of Scouting's and Guiding's founder, died aged 88. Her ashes were taken to Nyeri for burial next to B.-P.'s.

JUL 14 £101,525 was raised by the movement to purchase an off-shore lifeboat to mark the 150th anniversary of the Lifeboat Service in 1974. The lifeboat, named *Scout*, left Poole harbour and was formally accepted by Hartlepool Lifeboat station. 1974 is thought to be the first time that Scouts from Scotland, Wales, Northern Ireland and England have combined on a united fundraising project. The *Scout* was named in the presence of HM the Queen, the Chief Scout Sir William Gladstone, the Coventry Scout Band and many others, all listening to the familiar Gang Show song *We're riding along on the crest of a wave.* (The *Scout*, after 'retiring', went on to be manned by volunteers at a lifeboat station in Montevideo, Uruguay.)

NOV Former Chief Scout Lord Rowallan died (30th November).

1978 JUN £134,000 was donated to the Queen's Silver Jubilee Appeal through the sale of special joint Scout and Guide badges.

JUL Scouts appeared in the Royal Tournament for the first time with the Midlands Massed Scout Bands and a Field Gun display by the 4th Seven Kings Sea Scouts.

NOV At the request of the BBC, Scouts assisted the elderly in retuning their radios to new wavelengths.

DEC The 15th World Jamboree to be held in Iran was postponed.

1979 JAN Cub Scouts launched 'Cub Country' to aid community projects in

Nepal during International Year of the Child, eventually raising £165,000. Also, at the Great Children's Party in Hyde Park (in May), at 2 miles long, London Scouts cooked the world's longest sausage.

JUL As the 15th World Jamboree scheduled for Iran was postponed, international camps around the world, and 'Join-in-Jamborees', were held instead. Girl Guides took part in the Royal Tournament for the first time. Also, a World Scout Conference was held in Birmingham. 500 representatives from 81 countries present.

AUG Gilwell Park celebrated its 60th anniversary.

Earl Mountbatten, Commodore of Sea Scouts, was killed.

1980 MAR The National Air Activities Centre, Lasham, Hants, was closed due to rising costs.

World Scout membership was over 15 million (UK: 641, 281).

1981 FEB A memorial stone to the founder and Olave Lady Baden-Powell was unveiled in Westminster Abbey.

MAR 'Scouting and Unemployment' scheme introduced.

Scouts on duty on Royal Wedding route (Prince Charles and Lady Diana Spencer).

JUL 500 Venture Scouts acted as torch bearers at the Royal Fireworks Display, Hyde Park. *Scouting* monthly magazine cost 70p (£2.15 by 2003).

1982 JAN As part of 'The Year of the Scout' - celebrating 75 years of Scouting - 75 famous former Scouts gathered at the House of Commons to launch the special year.

FEB Major-General Michael Walsh became the new Chief Scout. The Isle of Man Post Office released a set of 5 stamps celebrating 75 years of Scouting.

MAR A commemorative 26p Scout stamp was issued by the Post Office (as part of Youth Movements issue). Special commemorative medallions were issued by the Tower Mint, one of which was a solid nickel and silver edition priced at £4.95. Other limited editions were available.

MAY 13 Death of 'Mr. Gang Show', Ralph Reader CBE.
The Queen unveiled a plaque at Hawkhirst Activity Centre. A reception was attended by former Chief Scout Lord Maclean, to mark the 21st anniversary of Baden-Powell House. Lastly, 250,000 Cubs took part in the fundraising National Cub Scout Tea-Making Fortnight.

JUN The 15th National Scout Band Festival was held at West Bromwich.

JUL Unipart National Scoutcar Races were held in Cleethorpes. Also, an international camp was held for Salvation Army Scouts and Guides at Walesby Forest, Nottingham.

AUG An international Sea Scout Camp was held in Ireland. Also, 1,500 Scouts from the UK and abroad took part in an international camp for able-bodied and handicapped Scouts. Called Extoree '82, it was held at Gilwell Park.

OCT The Beaver section was introduced for boys 6 - 8; it was not until

1986 that they became full members of the Scout Association, and were renamed Beaver Scouts (Beaver Scouts already operated in Northern Ireland; Canada had formally started a 5 - 7 Beaver programme in 1974). In 1982 HQ stated that the average size of a Scout Troop was 19 boys.

1983 JUL 15th World Jamboree held near Calgary, Canada.

1984 APR Cardinal Basil Hume preached at the National Scout Service, Windsor; the Duke of Kent reviewed 1,200 Queen's Scouts.
Also, Venture Scout Units visited Kenya and Sri Lanka in UNICEF's 'Decade of Clean Water' national project.
     SEP Gilwell Park's White House was closed due to its dangerous condition.

1985 JAN A friendship torch was carried from Baden-Powell House to Southampton by a Venture Scout relay team to kindle a friendship flame during the Mafeking centenary celebrations in South Africa.
     APR International Youth Year. New Scout training programme launched. Also in April, the Queen reviewed 1000 Queen's Scouts at Windsor (the Windsor review of King's/Queen's Scouts is an annual event started in 1934).

1986 JAN Guides' Rainbow Year. 70th Anniversary of Cubs.
     MAR 1,300 Venture Scouts took part in a Viking Venture in Denmark.
     MAY Woodland Scout campsite opened at National Garden Festival, Stoke-on-Trent.
     JUL The Duke of Kent reopened the 'B.-P. Story' exhibition to celebrate the 25th anniversary of Baden-Powell House.

1987 The Girl Guides launched Rainbow section for girls aged 5 - 7.
     MAR New Scottish HQ opened at Fordell Firs.
     JUN 250 Scouts from Greater London North East entered the *Guinness Book of Records* by cooking the world's longest sausage (nine miles). Also, 500 Venture Scouts assisted with the organisation of the St. John Ambulance Centenary Party in Hyde Park.
     JUL The 17th General Assembly of the International Fellowship of Former Scouts and Guides was held at the University of Warwick, attended by 700 members from 33 countries.
     AUG Service held on Brownsea Island (August 2nd) to mark the 80th anniversary of B.-P.'s experimental camp; Colonel Brian Evans-Lombe OBE, one of the original boy campers, attended.
     DEC The Duke of Kent attended the Birmingham Gang Show.
The 16th World Jamboree was held in Australia. Over 800 Scouts attended; the contingent included Ranger Guides for the first time.

1988 JAN The Venture Scout section began its 21st Anniversary Year.

The Sherpa '88 appeal was launched in aid of the Sherpa people.

    OCT William Garth Morrison, CBE, DL appointed the new Chief Scout.

1989 MAR London Venture, international camping weekend for 1,500 Swedish Senior Scouts and 3,500 British Venture Scouts at Crystal Palace. King Carl XVl Gustav of Sweden led the overseas visitors.

    APR First commercial sponsorship of a Scout proficiency badge. The Athlete badge was sponsored by 'Matchstick' Sportswear for three years.

    JUN Results of the Uniform Consultation Survey - the main change was the decision to abolish headgear for all sections.

    JUL 10,000 young people from over 40 countries attended the Discovery '89 Camps at five sites in the UK.

    OCT The 32nd International Jamboree-on-the-Air was held. A new amateur radio demonstration station, call-sign GB2GP, was opened at Gilwell Park.

    DEC The Scout Leadership Training Programme received an official commendation from the DOE in its National Training Awards Scheme.
Decision made to abolish all uniform headgear for all sections (except Sea Scouts).
Publication of a comprehensive biography of Baden-Powell by an historian from outside the movement -Tim Jeal. The first of its kind: a reliable and objective work, it is known today by many as the 'definitive book' on Baden-Powell.

1990 JAN 'Scouts Go For A Million' raised £141,998,67 for Barnardo's.
The Guide Association launched 'Action Plus', a new programme for those aged 13 - 16.

    FEB Girls could be admitted into the younger sections if Scout Groups wished. Girl Guides' new uniform, designed by Jeff Banks, was launched.

    JUN 'Green Charter' competition launched to raise awareness in environmental projects.

1991 JAN 75th anniversary of Cub Scouts; 50th anniversary of Air Scouts.

    FEB New Cub training programme was launched.

    APR HRH The Queen Mother reviewed Queen's Scouts at Windsor.

    JUL 170 children from Chernobyl area arrived in the UK for a holiday, hosted by British Scouts and Guides. Also, the Royal Charter changes were agreed so that girls could be allowed to be invested in the younger sections of the movement.

    AUG The 17th World Jamboree was held in South Korea; nearly 20,000 participants took part, the British contingent consisted of over 1,400 Scouts.

    NOV 2,000 Cubs took part in a 'Grand Howl' in Westminster; a Cubs' 75th Anniversary Thanksgiving Service was held in the Central Hall.

1992 Lord Baden-Powell (grandson of the founder) was appointed President of the Camping Club of Great Britain (the founder had been President in 1919).

    FEB A 'Promise Appeal' was launched, the first national fundraising appeal in aid of the movement since 1938.

OCT A National Woggle Day was held to raise funds for the Promise Appeal.

DEC The GSL/Commissioner Training scheme won a National Training Award from the Department of Employment. Also, the Promise Appeal raised approximately £2.5 million.

1993 The Scout and Cub Law was slightly altered as a consequence of the decision to admit girls to all sections.

SEP The founder's daughter, the Hon Mrs Betty Clay CBE, started the £2 million redevelopment programme at Gilwell Park to expand training facilities and restore/preserve the White House.

NOV The Cub and Scout Law was revised slightly as a consequence of the decision to admit girls to all the movement's sections.

1994 The Girl Guide Association was renamed 'The Guide Association'.

JAN Colonel Brian Evans-Lombe OBE, the only surviving member of the original Brownsea Island Camp, died aged 100.

JUL 'European Venture' took 6,000 Venture Scouts to Europe.

SEP The Gilwell Reunion celebrated 75 years of Gilwell Park.

NOV Gilwell's White House was reopened (not officially).

1995 JUN The Queen reopened the White House and refurbished Training Centre at Gilwell Park.

JUL The 18th World Jamboree was held in the Netherlands.

OCT 700 Scouts staged *In The Spotlight* at the Royal Albert Hall.

1996 MAR George Purdy was appointed as the new Chief Scout.

SEP Cubs celebrated 80 years of Cub Scouting with 80 days of special events, including a nationwide challenge to travel round the world in 80 days.

OCT The Scout Association website was launched: Scoutbase.org.uk.88
A £2 million scheme to refurbish Baden-Powell House/Hostel was launched.
The new Guide Law was introduced.

1997 FEB The Scout Association's Equal Opportunities Policy was announced.

SEP Scouts helped to clear away floral tributes left outside the royal palaces after the death of Princess Diana.

1998 FEB A 'Voice for Young People' policy was introduced to put young people under the age of 25 on all national committees. Also, a National Child Protection Coordinator was appointed for the Scout Association.

APR The S. A.'s Kosovo clothing appeal had overwhelming results.

MAY The World Scout Foundation reception was held at the Natural History Museum, London; attended by British and European royalty.
Jeans were made an official uniform option for Girl Guides.
DEC 1998 - JAN 1999 saw the 19th World Jamboree held in the Andean

foothills, Chile. The first-ever world Jamboree to be held in Latin America.

1999 APR The Scout Information Centre at Gilwell Park was opened.

JUN Twenty Scout and Guide Bands competed in the 23rd National Band Festival at Birmingham National Exhibition Centre.

JUL Britain was chosen to host the 2007 World Jamboree by the World Scout Conference meeting in Durban, South Africa.

OCT The S.A. faced financial difficulties, resulting in job losses and reorganisation of roles. All Headquarters departments co-located to Gilwell Park (except Scout Shops Ltd).

2000 MAY Millennium Camps held by Scout Groups throughout the UK (due to a weekend of torrential rain, many were flooded out and had to be abandoned!).

JUL A major uniform consultation exercise was undertaken.

DEC The Headquarters part of Baden-Powell House was closed and sold off. The movement appointed its first female editor for its monthly magazine.

2001 FEB The movement's new logo was launched, and also the proposed new uniform was launched during London fashion week.

APR   The Duke of Kent opened Gilwell House (the new Scout Association office building at Gilwell Park).

2002 Launch of new Scout uniforms, sections and training programmes. 'Girl' gets back into the Guides' title, the Guide Association became Girlguiding UK.
DEC 2002 - JAN 2003: 20th World Jamboree held in Thailand with over 24,000 Scouts.

2003 Sophie, Countess of Wessex, was appointed President of the UK Girl Guide movement.

JUN In Channel 4's *Big Brother* reality show, housemates were made 'honorary' Cubs. They wore the uniform and had to do numerous Cub tasks.

2004 JAN 90th Birthday of Brownies.

MAR A new edition of *Scouting for Boys* was published by OUP.

APR The Hon Mrs Betty Clay CBE, the B.-P.s' last surviving daughter, died on April 24th.

SEP Former *Blue Peter* presenter, Peter Duncan, was invested as the new (ninth) Chief Scout. Also, the last edition of *Scouting* magazine was published in its monthly/size A4 format.

NOV Scout Shop branches ceased trading, taken over by Blacks Ltd.

2005 MAY An inaugural Muslim Scout Fellowship Camp was held at Youlbury Scout campsite, Oxford.

JUL/AUG Eurojam held in Hylands Park, Chelmsford, Essex. Attended by

10,000 Scouts and Guides from Britain and Europe.

AUG Having won £15 million on the lottery, husband and wife Scouters, Paul and Thea Bristow of the 1st Torbay Group, treated Cubs, Scouts and parents to a two weeks' activities holiday in Egmont, Canada. An entire Boeing 767 was chartered by the Bristows.

2006 JAN 90th Birthday of Guides' Senior section (formerly called Rangers). The Guides' 2006 census recorded a total UK membership of 533,466; total number of UK Guides (ages 10 -15) was 123,785.
There were fifteen registered Muslim Scout Groups in the UK, and ten more were said to be in the process of opening.

2007 Total membership of The Scout Association, 2007, including all members - children and adults - 818,963. The Scout movement's Centenary - numerous celebrations and media reports/programmes. The Royal Mint circulated a new 50p coin with the Scout emblem, designed by Kerry Jones. **26th MAY:** Centenary camps held by Scout Groups all over the UK; **JUL:** the Royal Mail issued six new stamps to celebrate the centenary; **AUG:** 21st World Jamboree - 'One World, One Promise'- with over 40,000 attending the Jamboree at Hylands Park, Chelmsford, Essex; Brownsea: special Sunrise Camp and many other celebrations...

BIBLIOGRAPHY

Baden-Powell, The Hero of Mafeking, Aitken, W. Francis, London 1900

Window on my Heart, Baden-Powell, Olave, London 1973

Lessons From The Varsity of Life, Baden-Powell, Robert, London 1933

B.-P.'s Scouts: An Official History of the Boy Scouts Association, Collis, Henry with Hurll, Fred and Hazlewood, Rex, London 1961

The John Hassall Lifestyle, Cuppleditch, David, London 1979

The First Ten Years, Everett, Percy 1948

Shackleton, Fisher, M and J, London 1957

Legalised Mischief, The History of the Scout Movement From a Grassroots Perspective, Harris, Steven, London 2002

Baden-Powell: The Two Lives of a Hero, Hillcourt, William with Baden-Powell, Olave, 1964

Baden-Powell, Jeal, Tim, 1989

Don Potter: An Inspiring Century, Light, Vivienne, 2002

Lone Scout ~ W. D. Boyce and American Boy Scouting, Petterchak, Janice, USA, 2003

Charterhouse, A History of the School, Quick, Anthony, London 1990

An Ordinary Troop, Reeves, A, Devon, 1992

The Piper of Pax, Wade, E.K., London 1924

Olave Baden-Powell, The Authorised Biography, Wade, E.K., London 1971

Treetops Hotel, Walker, Eric, London 1962

C.B. Fry, An English Hero, Wilton, Iain, London 1999

ACKNOWLEDGEMENTS

Sincere thanks go to Professor Barry Fantoni for permission to use an image of his painting of Baden-Powell on the front cover. I am also indebted to Lord Baden-Powell, Robin Clay and members of the extended Baden-Powell family for their kind support and help with research and material. Similarly, I am indebted to John Roberts and Hazel Constance, who have kindly given of their time to help with proof reading. I am also grateful to Tim Jeal and his publishers Pimlico for permission to use extracts from his biography of Baden-Powell.

Additionally, the following institutions/organisations and people generously helped by providing images, or contributed time, material and resources, all of which helped the author immeasurably: the British Library, Scott Polar Research Centre, Norman Plastow and the Wimbledon Windmill Trust, the Camping and Caravanning Club archives, the National Trust, The Scout Association, Girlguiding UK, Daily Telegraph, The Times, The Scouter/Scouting magazine, Associated Press, Royal borough of Kensington and Chelsea Library and Local Studies Centre, the Royal Mint, Ann Wheeler and Charterhouse School, George Tyson and Rose Hill School, MJS Harris - headmaster of Sandroyd School, the Army Museum, the Wimbledon and Putney Commons Conservators, Bodlian Library, Poole Historical Trust, Leslie Holmes and the Salford Lads' Club, Christopher Lumgair and the London Sketch Club, the archives and records department of the Natural History Museum, Bailey Brothers and Swinfen publishers, Michael Loomes and the Story of Scouting Museum, Alan Shrimpton and Bryanston School, True's Yard Fishing Heritage Museum, John Mackintosh and the 1st Godstone Scout Group, Anne Davidson, Chris Matuszek, Gil Fuqua, David Johnson, Doug Ramsey and the 3rd Bromley Scout Group, Graeme Jones, Andrew Neden, Jack Olden, Roy Masini, Bob Gammon, David McCleave, Dr Stephan Schrolkamp, Peter Moore, Gary Haines and the Mercers' Company archives, Steven Williams and Slapstick Design Partnership, Suzanne Sieger.

For a detailed history of the birth and development of the UK Scout movement, decade by decade, see the author's series Legalised Mischief (Lewarne Publishing).